MW00352534

The Big Ninja Foodi Cookbook

1000-Days Easy & Delicious Ninja Foodi Pressure Cooker and Air Fryer Recipes
for Beginners and Advanced Users

Myrtle Barker

© Copyright 2021 - All rights reserved

This document is geared towards providing exact and reliable information with regards to the topic and issue covered. The publication is sold with the idea that the publisher is not required to render accounting, officially permitted, or otherwise, qualified services. If advice is necessary, legal, or professional, a practiced individual in the profession should be ordered. - From a Declaration of Principles which was accepted and approved equally by a Committee of the American Bar Association and a Committee of Publishers and Associations. In no way is it legal to reproduce, duplicate, or transmit any part of this document in either electronic means or in printed format. Recording of this publication is strictly prohibited and any storage of this document is not allowed unless with written permission from the publisher.

All rights reserved. The information provided herein is stated to be truthful and consistent, in that any liability, in terms of inattention or otherwise, by any usage or abuse of any policies, processes, or directions contained within is the solitary and utter responsibility of the recipient reader.

Under no circumstances will any legal responsibility or blame be held against the publisher for any reparation, damages, or monetary loss due to the information herein, either directly or indirectly. Respective authors own all copyrights not held by the publisher.

The information herein is offered for informational purposes solely, and is universal as so. The presentation of the information is without contract or any type of guarantee assurance. The trademarks that are used are without any consent, and the publication of the trademark is without permission or backing by the trademark owner.

All trademarks and brands within this book are for clarifying purposes only and are the owned by the owners themselves, not affiliated with this document.

TABLE OF CONTENTS

Introduction

Ninja Foodi has just raised the bars and turned cooking into a quality experience with its fine appliances. The Ninja food multi-purpose cooker has taken center stage for its range of cooking options and the ultra-convenience it offers to the users. A pressure cooker, Ninja Foodi also offers crispy air frying and slow cooking options. The structural built of this intelligent device gives enough space to meet the needs of each serving size. All the recipes shared over the text of this book highlight the potential of this appliance, covering from breakfast meals to the crispy snacks, meat, vegetables and dessert, Ninja Foodi can assist in quick cooking with it a multi-functioning operating system. Say goodbye to uneven cooking or burning of the food.

Features of a Ninja Foodi

There several cooking functions that are given in a Ninja Foodi. These modes are enough to meet the daily cooking needs of a person. From saucy meals to crispy delights, everything can be cooked inside this closed vessel. The control panel of Ninja Foodi clearly shows all the modes provided. When you select a specific function, the device automatically sets its temperature and pressure accordingly. Moreover, there is a manual operation that allows us to operate the device as per the desired settings. More often than usual, Manual settings are used for cooking the meal in an electric cooker.

A single base unit of ninja Foodi multipurpose cooker can carry out several functions. In this single vessel, you can try all the following functions:

PRESSURE COOKING

By pressing the Pressure Cook button, you can switch the device to this mode. A pressure lid is used to maintain the internal pressure. The pressure release valve on top of the lid should be turned to 'Sealed' position to avoid leakage. Once this operation has been carried, you can turn the pressure released handle to the 'venting' position to release the steam quickly.

STEAMING

A Foodi can also be turned into a steamer by selecting "steam' mode and pouring water into the pot. Set the reversible rack into the Ninja Foodi's pot and keep the items for steaming over it. Now cover the lid while securing the pressure valve and press 'Start.' After the operation, release steam and enjoy the food.

SLOW COOKING

You can turn your Ninja Foodi into a Slow Cook and works exactly like a crockpot. Just add the ingredients and cover the lid without sealing the valves. Set the Slow cook mode, temperature and time.

AIR CRISPING

To add crisp to the food, Foodi gives you "Air Crisp" cooking mode. It has a separate Air Crisp basket and a crisper basket. Add food to the basket and attach its handle to place it in the Foodi. Remove the handles and Close the Ninja's lid. Press Air Crisp and adjust time and temperature.

BAKING/ ROASTING

A single button allows two functions in the Ninja Foodi. You can bake and roast anything. For cakes, you need to place the rack inside and then keep the baking pan over it.

BROILING

Ninja Foodi can mimic the function of a broiler by its broil mode. When food is cooked in this mode, it is heated from the top to bring more color to the food. Place the reversible rack in the Ninja Foodi insert and cover the lid. Press the broil button and adjust the time and temperature according. Once done, press the stop button and remove the lid.

DEHYDRATING

Buying a dehydrator separately is not convenient for everybody. The Ninja Foodi has brought great ease in this regard as it gives a unique option to dehydrate any ingredient in the same vessel. It is carried out for a long duration at low temperatures. A double layer Cook and Crisp basket are placed in the Foodi, and the items are placed in it. select Dehydrate after closing the lid, and the device will do rest.

SEARING/SAUTEING

The sauté mode allows cooking without the lid. It simply heats up the base of the cooking pot just enough to sear or sauté it in little or no oil. To carry out this function. Simply preheat the device on this mode and add the cooking fats to the insert. Let it warm up, and then toss in the ingredients for sautéing. Normally vegetables are sautéed at this mode, or the meat is seared. This mode is not good for the complete tenderizing of the ingredients but only to cook them lightly from the outside.

Tips for Using the Ninja Foodi

The Ninja Foodi, with all its preset functions, can help the newbies to cook directly without messing with timing and temperature. The control panel clearly states each function while displaying the ongoing operation, the timer and the temperature set on the device. The control panel has a soft touch system which keeps it convenient to use for every function.

Fix the Condensation collector:

The steam or condensation collector is an important part of every closed cooking vessel. This comes with every other electric Ninja Foodi, including the Ninja Foodi. There is a separate place for condensation collector, which is at the side of the base unit. The collector is fixed into its given place. Once fixed, it can be removed again easily. After each cooking session, this collector must be emptied first and wash well. When it clean and dry, put the collector back in its place.

Put the Ingredients into the Ninja Foodi's pot:

Every Ninja Foodi cooker comes with a base unit containing a removable cooking pot or inserts inside it. This is the insert that holds the food while it is cooked in Ninja Foodi. Everything must be placed in it before cooking. If you are steaming any food, then the insert is filled with water, and the insert basket or trivet is placed inside; on this basket, the food places. For air crisping, a crisper basket is placed into the Ninja Foodi's pot. This insert can even hold small-sized ramekins or baking pans when required. The insert has these markings, which can be used to check the level of the content. It also states the maximum limit, which 2/3 of the full. The level of the food should reach above this limit.

Close the Ninja's lid:

Except for sautéing and searing, all other cooking options in the Ninja Foodi Requires closing of the lid, especially for steaming, baking and pressure cooking. The lid should not only be closed, but it also needs to be locked completely to seal the cooking vessel. After placing the cooking pot, cover the lid of the base. When you place the lid back on, the "arrow" mark on the lid and the 'unlock' mark of the cooker base align. Now twist the lid counterclockwise until it clicks, and the 'lock' mark on the base and lid will align. Gently press down the float valve to ensure secure locking. If the lid is not closed tightly, then the cooker will not function. Do not airtight the vessel with the lid while the cooker is on 'sauté,' slow cook, keep warm mode. Keep the lid open, meanwhile.

Pressure release and Float Valve:

This step is important for methods that involve cooking at specialized pressures. The pressure release handle loosely rests on the pressure release outlet and rotate between 'sealed position' and 'venting position.' The handle can also be removed for cleaning. For pressure cooking, the "end" of this button has to be pointed towards the "sealed position." Make sure to adjust the pressure release button right after locking the lid. Remember each mode except "Sauté" and "Keep Warm," slow cook, requires sealing of the pressure release valve. Ensure that the float valve is also resting in the downward position. For Slow cook and keep warm mode, remember to turn the release valve to "venting position" right after covering the lid. To sauté, do not cover the lid.

Select from the Cooking Options:

As Ninja Foodi cooker provides you with a range of cooking modes, each mode has its own custom setting to adjust the pressure and time accordingly. To initiate cooking, press any of the operation keys for the desired program. Remember, each operation has its own settings, but if you want to add changes to the time and pressure, then use the operational button to do so. A standard control panel gives you the following options for cooking:

1. Slow Cook
2. Pressure Cook
3. Air Crisp
4. Bake/ Roast
5. Steam
6. Dehydrate
7. Manual
8. Sauté/ Sear

After the mode selection, your cooker will automatically switch to the Preheating State within 10seconds. During the preheating stage, the cooker will build up the internal pressure and then finally switch to the cooking state.

Time and pressure Adjustment:

Besides the present options, the Ninja Food multipurpose cooker also gives you a 'Manual' operation where you can adjust the time, pressure and even temperature as per the demand of the recipe. There is a separate key to adjust these functions. You can either increase or decrease the set time and temperature and select any of the pressure options. Usually, it is the high pressure on which the pressure cooking is carried out. The appliance takes its time to reach the selected temperature; the timer starts ticking once that temperature is achieved.

Once everything is adjusted well as per the desired settings, the final stage is to initiate cooking by pressing the Start/Stop button on the button panel of the base unit. If you are pressure cooking the food, make sure to turn the pressure release handle first to the closed position. Likewise, at the end of the operation, the pressure released handle must be turned towards the venting position in order to quickly release all the steam inside. Another method is to leave the device for 20 minutes, and the steam will automatically release out of the cooker through its condensation collector channel.

Unlock and Remove the lid:

When the steam inside the cooker is completely released, the lid can be removed. Leave the device for 15 minutes at least to naturally release the pressure. To confirm if the pressure is completely released, using the pressure handle and turn it to the venting position. Any remaining steam will also pass out through this way. Unlock the lid and remove it while keeping your head away from the top of the cooker. Such care is needed to avoid any accidental steam burns. Use a long-handled spoon to stir the ingredients inside, then serve out the meal. Handle the lid only through its handles and avoid touching directly any part of it.

Chapter 1-Breakfast Recipes

Sausage Cheese Frittata

Prep Time: 15 minutes

Cooking time: 20 minutes

Servings: 2

Ingredients:

- 1/4 lb. breakfast sausage, cooked and crumbled
- 4 eggs, beaten
- 1/2 cup cheddar cheese, shredded
- 1 red bell pepper, diced
- 1 green onion, chopped
- Cooking spray

Directions:

1. Mix the eggs, sausage, cheese, onion and bell pepper.
2. Spray a small baking pan with oil. Pour the egg mixture into the pan.
3. Set the basket inside the Ninja Foodi. Close the crisping lid.
4. Select "Air Crisp" cooking mode. Cook at 360 degrees F temperature for almost 20 minutes.
5. Serve warm.

Nutrition Values Per Serving:

Calories: 380, Total fat: 27.4g, Carbohydrates: 2.9g, Protein: 31.2g

Butter Dipped Broccoli Florets

Prep Time: 10 minutes

Cooking time: 8 minutes

Servings: 4

Ingredients:

- 4 tablespoons butter
- Salt and black pepper, to taste
- 2 pounds broccoli florets
- 1 cup whip cream

Directions:

1. Arrange basket in the bottom of your Ninja Foodi and add water
2. Place florets on top of the basket. Lock the Ninja Foodi's lid and cook on "Pressure" mode at High for 5 minutes
3. Quick-release pressure and transfer florets to the pot itself
4. Season with salt, pepper and add butter
5. Lock the Crisping Lid and Air Crisp on 360 degrees F 3 minutes
6. Transfer to a serving plate.
7. Serve and enjoy!

Nutrition Values Per Serving:

Calories: 178, Total fat: 4g, Carbohydrates: 8g, Protein: 6g

Egg Turkey Cups

Prep Time: 10 minutes

Cooking time: 10 minutes

Servings: 4

Ingredients:

- 8 tablespoons turkey sausage, cooked and crumbled, divided
- 8 tablespoons frozen spinach, chopped and divided
- 8 teaspoons shredded cheddar cheese, divided
- 4 eggs

Directions:

1. Add a layer of the sausage, spinach and cheese on each muffin cup.
2. Crack the egg open on top. Seal the crisping lid. Select "Air Crisp" cooking mode.
3. Cook at 330 degrees F temperature for almost 10 minutes.
4. Serve warm.

Nutrition Values Per Serving:

Calories: 171, Total fat: 13.3g, Carbohydrates: 0.5g, Protein: 11.9g

Roasted Potatoes

Prep Time: 30 minutes

Cooking time: 20 minutes

Servings: 6

Ingredients:

- 2 lb. baby potatoes, sliced into wedges
- 2 tablespoons olive oil
- 2 teaspoons garlic salt

Directions:

1. Toss the potatoes in olive oil and garlic salt.
2. Add the potatoes to the Ninja Foodi Air Fryer's insert.
3. Seal the crisping lid. Select "Air Crisp" cooking mode.
4. Cook at 390 degrees F temperature for almost 20 minutes.
5. Serve warm.

Nutrition Values Per Serving:

Calories: 131, Total fat: 4.8g, Carbohydrates: 20 g, Protein: 4.1g

Broccoli Quiche

Prep Time: 20 minutes

Cooking time: 22 minutes

Servings: 2

Ingredients:

- 1 cup of water
- 2 cups broccoli florets

- 1 carrot, chopped
- 1 cup cheddar cheese, grated
- 1/4 cup Feta cheese, crumbled
- 1/4 cup milk
- 2 eggs
- 1 teaspoon parsley
- 1 teaspoon thyme
- Salt and black pepper, to taste

Directions:

1. Pour the water inside the Ninja Foodi. Place the basket inside.
2. Put the carrots and broccoli in the Ninja Foodi. Cover the cooker with the lid.
3. Set it to "Pressure" cooking mode. Cook at high pressure for 2 minutes.
4. Release the pressure quickly. Crack all the eggs in a suitable bowl and beat.
5. For seasoning, add salt, pepper, parsley and thyme.
6. Put the vegetables on a small baking pan.
7. Layer with the cheese and pour in the beaten eggs Place in the Ninja Foodi.
8. Select "Air Crisp" cooking mode. Seal the crisping lid.
9. Cook at 350 degrees F temperature for almost 20 minutes.
10. Enjoy

Nutrition Values Per Serving:

Calories: 401, Total fat: 28g, Carbohydrates: 13g, Protein: 26g

Egg Burrito

Prep Time: 10 minutes

Cooking time: 10 minutes

Servings: 8

Ingredients:

- 3 eggs, beaten
- Salt and black pepper, to taste
- Cooking spray
- 8 tortillas
- 2 red bell peppers, julienned
- 1 onion, sliced

Directions:

1. Beat the eggs in a suitable bowl.
2. For seasoning, add salt and black pepper. Set aside.
3. Select sauté mode on the Ninja Foodi. Spray with the oil.
4. Cook the vegetables until soft. Remove and set aside.
5. Pour the eggs into the pot. Cook until firm.
6. Wrap the eggs and veggies with a tortilla.
7. Serve warm.

Nutrition Values Per Serving:

Calories: 92, Total fat: 2.5g, Carbohydrates: 14.4g, Protein: 3.9g

Bacon Egg Scramble

Prep Time: 10 minutes

Cooking time: 5 minutes

Servings: 2

Ingredients:

- 4 strips bacon
- 2 eggs
- 1 tablespoon milk
- Salt and black pepper, to taste

Directions:

1. Place the bacon inside the Ninja Foodi. Select "Air Crisp" cooking mode.
2. Cover the crisping lid. Cook at 390 degrees F temperature for almost 3 minutes.
3. Flip and cook for another 2 minutes. Remove the bacon and set it aside.
4. Whisk the eggs and milk in a suitable bowl. For seasoning, add salt and black pepper.
5. Set the Ninja Foodi to sauté. Add the eggs and cook until firm.
6. Serve warm.

Nutrition Values Per Serving:

Calories: 272, Total fat: 20.4g, Carbohydrates: 1.3g, Protein: 20g

Mushroom Omelets

Prep Time: 15 minutes

Cooking time: 8 minutes

Servings: 2

Ingredients:

- 2 eggs
- 1/4 cup milk
- 1 tablespoon red bell pepper, chopped
- 1 slice ham, diced
- 1 tablespoon mushrooms, chopped
- Salt to taste
- 1/4 cup cheese, shredded

Directions:

1. Whisk the eggs and milk in a suitable bowl. Add the ham and vegetables. For seasoning, add the salt.

2. Pour the mixture into a small pan. Place the pan inside the Ninja Foodi Air Fryer's insert.

3. Seal the crisping lid. Select "Air Crisp" cooking mode. Cook at 350 degrees F temperature for almost 8 minutes.

4. Before it is fully cooked, sprinkle the cheese on top.

5. Serve warm.

Nutrition Values Per Serving:

Calories: 177, Total fat: 11g, Carbohydrates: 7.1g, Protein: 13.1g

Paprika Shrimp

Prep Time: 10 minutes

Cooking time: 15 minutes

Servings: 4

Ingredients:

- 2 tablespoons butter
- 1/2 teaspoon smoked paprika
- 1-pound shrimps, peeled and deveined
- Lemongrass stalks
- 1 red Chilli pepper, seeded and chopped

Directions:

1. Take a suitable bowl and mix all of the ingredients well, except lemongrass and marinate for 1 hour

2. Transfer to Ninja Foodi and Lock the Ninja Foodi's lid, cook on "Bake/Roast" cooking mode for 15 minutes at 345 degrees F

3. Once done, serve and enjoy!

Nutrition Values Per Serving:

Calories: 251, Total fat: 10g, Carbohydrates: 3g, Protein: 34g

Egg Scramble

Prep Time: 10 minutes

Cooking time: 5-10 minutes

Servings: 2

Ingredients:

- 4 strips bacon
- 2 whole eggs
- 1 tablespoon milk
- Salt and black pepper, to taste

Directions:

1. Add bacon inside your Ninja Foodi.
2. Lock the Crisping Lid and Select "Air Crisp" cooking mode.
3. Cook for 3 minutes at 390 degrees F. Flip and cook for 2 minutes more
4. Remove bacon and keep it on the side. Take a suitable bowl and whisk in eggs and milk
5. Season with salt and black pepper. Set your Ninja Foodi to Sauté mode.
6. Add eggs, cook until firm.
7. Serve and enjoy!

Nutrition Values Per Serving:

Calories: 272, Total fat: 20g, Carbohydrates: 1g, Protein: 19g

Crispy Broccoli Florets

Prep Time: 10 minutes

Cooking time: 5 minutes

Servings: 4

Ingredients:

- 4 tablespoons butter, melted
- Salt and black pepper, to taste
- 2 pounds broccoli florets
- 1 cup whipping cream

Directions:

1. Place a steamer basket in your Ninja Foodi's insert and add water
2. Place florets on top of the basket and Lock the Ninja Foodi's lid
3. Cook on "Pressure" mode at High for 5 minutes. Quick-release pressure
4. Transfer florets from the steamer basket to the pot. Add salt, pepper, butter, and stir
5. Lock the Crisping Lid and cook on "Air Crisp" cooking mode for 360 degrees F.
6. Serve and enjoy!

Nutrition Values Per Serving:

Calories: 178, Total fat: 14g, Carbohydrates: 8g, Protein: 5g

Carrot Meal

Prep Time: 10 minutes

Cooking time: 4 minutes

Servings: 4

Ingredients:

- 1 and a 1/2-pound carrots, chopped
- 1 tablespoon of butter at room temperature
- 1 tablespoon of agave nectar
- 1/4 teaspoon of sea salt
- 1 cup of water

Directions:

1. Clean and peel your carrots properly. Roughly chop them into small pieces
2. Pour 1 cup of water into Ninja Foodi's cooking pot.
3. Place the carrots in a steamer basket and place the basket in the Ninja Foodi
4. Seal the Ninja's lid and cook on "Pressure" mode at High for 4 minutes. Do a quick release to remove the steam.
5. Transfer the carrots to a deep bowl and use an immersion blender to blend the carrots
6. Add butter, nectar, salt, and puree. Taste the puree and season more if needed.
7. Enjoy!

Nutrition Values Per Serving:

Calories: 143, Total fat: 9g, Carbohydrates: 16g, Protein: 2g

Avocado Stuffed Eggs

Prep Time: 10 minutes

Cooking time: 5 minutes

Servings: 6

Ingredients:

- 1/2 tablespoon fresh lemon juice

- 1 medium ripe avocado, peeled, pitted and chopped
- 6 eggs, boiled, peeled and cut in half lengthwise
- Salt to taste
- 1/2 cup fresh watercress, trimmed

Directions:

1. Place steamer basket at the bottom of your Ninja Foodi. Add water
2. Add watercress on the basket and Lock the Ninja Foodi's lid.
3. Cook on "Pressure" mode at High for almost 3 minutes, then quick release the pressure and drain the watercress
4. Remove egg yolks and transfer them to a suitable bowl
5. Add watercress, avocado, lemon juice, salt into the bowl and mash with a fork
6. Place egg whites in a serving bowl and fill them with the watercress and avocado dish.
7. Serve!

Nutrition Values Per Serving:

Calories: 132, Total fat: 10g, Carbohydrates: 3g, Protein: 5g

Avocado Egg Cups

Prep Time: 30 minutes

Cooking time: 15 minutes

Servings: 2

Ingredients:

- 1 avocado, sliced in half and pitted
- 2 eggs
- Salt and black pepper, to taste
- 1/4 cup cheddar, shredded

Directions:

1. Crack the egg into the avocado slice.
2. For seasoning, add salt and black pepper.
3. Put it on the Ninja Foodi Air Fryer's insert. Seal the crisping lid.
4. Select "Air Crisp" cooking mode. Cook at 400 degrees F temperature for almost 15 minutes.
5. Sprinkle with the cheese 3 minutes before it is cooked.
6. Serve warm.

Nutrition Values Per Serving:

Calories: 281, Total fat: 23g, Carbohydrates: 9g, Protein: 11g

Crispy Egg Toast

Prep Time: 15 minutes

Cooking time: 9 minutes

Servings: 1

Ingredients:

- 1 slice bread

- 1 egg
- Salt and black pepper, to taste
- Cooking spray

Directions:

1. Spray a small baking pan with oil. Place the bread inside the pan.
2. Make a medium-sized hole in the center of the bread slice.
3. Crack open the egg and put it inside the hole.
4. Cover the Ninja Foodi with the crisping lid. Select "Air Crisp" cooking mode.
5. Cook at 330 degrees F temperature for almost 6 minutes. Flip the toast and cook for 3 more minutes.
6. Serve warm.

Nutrition Values Per Serving:

Calories: 92, Total fat: 5.2g, Carbohydrates: 5g, Protein: 6.2g

Herbed Eggs

Prep Time: 10 minutes

Cooking time: 5 minutes

Servings: 1

Ingredients:

- Cooking spray
- 1 egg
- 1 teaspoon dried rosemary
- Salt and black pepper, to taste

Directions:

1. Coat a ramekin with oil. Crack the egg into the ramekin.
2. For seasoning, add rosemary, salt and black pepper.
3. Close the crisping lid. Select "Air Crisp" cooking mode.
4. Cook at 330 degrees F temperature for almost 5 minutes.
5. Serve warm.

Nutrition Values Per Serving:

Calories: 72, Total fat: 5.1g, Carbohydrates: 1.2g, Protein: 5.6g

Cheesy Herb Frittata

Prep Time: 15 minutes

Cooking time: 15 minutes

Servings: 4

Ingredients:

- 4 eggs
- 1/2 cup half and half
- 2 tablespoons parsley, chopped
- 2 tablespoons chives, chopped

- 1/4 cup shredded cheddar cheese
- Salt and black pepper, to taste

Directions:

1. Beat the eggs in a suitable bowl. Add the rest of the ingredients and stir well.
2. Pour the mixture into a small baking pan.
3. Place the pan on top of the Ninja Foodi Air Fryer's insert.
4. Seal the crisping lid. Select "Air Crisp" cooking mode.
5. Cook at 330 degrees F temperature for almost 15 minutes.
6. Serve warm.

Nutrition Values Per Serving:

Calories: 132, Total fat: 10.2g, Carbohydrates: 1.9g, Protein: 8.3g

Zested Lamb Chops

Prep Time: 5 minutes

Cooking time: 40 minutes

Servings: 4

Ingredients:

- 4 tablespoons butter
- 3 tablespoons lemon juice
- 4 lamb chops, with bone
- 2 tablespoons flour
- 1 cup Picante sauce

Directions:

1. Coat chops with flour, keep them on the side
2. Set your Ninja Foodi to Sauté mode and add butter, chops
3. Sauté for 2 minutes, add Picante sauce and lemon juice
4. Lock the Ninja Foodi's lid and cook on "Pressure" mode at High for 40 minutes.
5. Release the pressure naturally and serve.

Nutrition Values Per Serving:

Calories: 284, Total fat: 20g, Carbohydrates: 1g, Protein: 24g

Butter Salmon

Prep Time: 10 minutes

Cooking time: 30 minutes

Servings: 6

Ingredients:

- 1-pound salmon fillets
- 2 tablespoons ginger/garlic paste
- 3 green chilies, chopped
- Salt and black pepper, to taste
- 3/4 cup butter

Directions:

1. Season salmon fillets with ginger, garlic paste, salt, pepper
2. Place salmon fillets to Ninja Foodi and top with green chilies and butter
3. Lock the Ninja Foodi's lid and cook on the "Bake/Roast" cooking mode for 30 minutes at 360 degrees F
4. Enjoy!

Nutrition Values Per Serving:

Calories: 507, Total fat: 45g, Carbohydrates: 3g, Protein: 22g

Hash Brown Casserole

Prep Time: 10 minutes

Cooking time: 20 minutes

Servings: 4

Ingredients:

- Cooking spray
- 1 lb. hash browns
- 1 lb. breakfast sausage, cooked and crumbled
- 1 red bell pepper, diced
- 1 green bell pepper, diced
- 1 onion, diced
- 4 eggs
- Salt and black pepper, to taste

Directions:

1. Coat a small baking pan with oil. Place the hash browns on the bottom part.
2. Add the sausage and then the onion and bell peppers.
3. Place the pan on top of the Ninja Foodi basket. Put the basket inside the pot.
4. Close the crisping lid. Select "Air Crisp" cooking mode. Cook at 350 degrees F temperature for almost 10 minutes.
5. Open the lid. Crack the eggs on top. Cook for another 10 minutes on Saute mode.
6. For seasoning, add salt and black pepper.
7. Serve warm.

Nutrition Values Per Serving:

Calories: 513, Total fat: 34g, Carbohydrates: 30g, Protein: 21.1g

Fried Eggs

Prep Time: 5 minutes

Cooking time: 10 minutes

Servings: 2

Ingredients:

- 4 eggs
- 1/4 teaspoon black pepper
- 1 teaspoon butter, melted
- 3/4 teaspoon salt

Directions:

1. Take a small egg pan and brush it with butter.
2. Beat the eggs in the pan and sprinkle with the black pepper and salt.
3. Transfer the egg pan into the Ninja Foodi's pot.
4. Cover the Ninja Foodi's lid. Cook the meat for 10 minutes at 350 degrees F.
5. Serve immediately and enjoy!

Nutrition Values Per Serving:

Calories: 143, Total fat: 10.2g, Carbohydrates: 0.9g, Protein: 11.4g

Tofu with Mushrooms

Prep Time: 10 minutes

Cooking time: 10 minutes

Servings: 2

Ingredients:

- 8 tablespoons parmesan cheese, shredded
- 2 cups fresh mushrooms, chopped
- 2 blocks tofu, pressed and cubed
- Salt and black pepper, to taste
- 8 tablespoons butter

Directions:

1. Take a suitable bowl and mix in tofu, salt, and pepper
2. Set your Ninja Foodi to Sauté mode and add seasoned tofu, Sauté for 5 minutes
3. Add mushroom, cheese and Sauté for 3 minutes.
4. Lock the crisping lid and cook on the "Air Crisp" mode for 3 minutes at 350 degrees F.
5. Transfer to a serving plate and enjoy!

Nutrition Values Per Serving:

Calories: 211, Total fat: 18g, Carbohydrates: 2g, Protein: 11g

Mushroom Stir Fry

Prep Time: 10 minutes

Cooking time: 15 minutes

Servings: 8

Ingredients:

- 1-pound white mushrooms stems trimmed
- 2 tablespoons unsalted butter
- 1/2 teaspoon salt
- 1/4 cup of water

Directions:

1. Quarter medium mushrooms and cut any large mushrooms into eight
2. Put mushrooms, butter, and salt in your Foodi's inner pot
3. Add water and lock pressure lid, making sure to seal the valve
4. Cook on "Pressure" mode at High for 5 minutes, quick release pressure once did
5. Once done, set your pot to Sauté mode on HIGH mode and bring the mix to a boil over 5 minutes until all the water evaporates
6. Once the liquid has evaporated, stir for 1 minute until slightly browned.

7.   Enjoy!

Nutrition Values Per Serving:

Calories: 50, Total fat: 4g, Carbohydrates: 2g, Protein: 2g

Soupy Lamb Roast

Prep Time: 10 minutes

Cooking time: 60 minutes

Servings: 6

Ingredients:

*   2 pounds lamb roast
*   1 cup onion soup
*   1 cup beef broth
*   Salt and black pepper, to taste

Directions:

1.   Transfer lamb roast to your Ninja Foodi pot.
2.   Add onion soup, beef broth, salt, and pepper on top.
3.   Lock the Ninja Foodi's lid and cook on Medium-HIGH pressure for 55 minutes.
4.   Release pressure naturally over 10 minutes.
5.   Transfer to a serving bowl and serve!

Nutrition Values Per Serving:

Calories: 349, Total fat: 18g, Carbohydrates: 2.9g, Protein: 39g

Morning Sausage Meal

Prep Time: 10 minutes

Cooking time: 20 minutes

Servings: 6

Ingredients:

*   4 whole eggs
*   4 sausages, cooked and sliced
*   2 tablespoons butter
*   1/2 cup mozzarella cheese, grated
*   1/2 cup cream

Directions:

1.   Take a suitable bowl and mix everything
2.   Add egg mix to your Ninja Foodi, top with cheese and sausage slices
3.   Lock pressure lid and select "BAKE/ROAST" mode and cook for 20 minutes at 345 degrees F
4.   Serve and enjoy!

Nutrition Values Per Serving:

Calories: 180, Total fat: 12g, Carbohydrates: 4g, Protein: 12g

Cinnamon French Toast

Prep Time: 15 minutes

Cooking time: 10 minutes

Servings: 2

Ingredients:

*   2 eggs, beaten
*   1/4 cup milk

- 1/4 cup brown sugar
- 1 tablespoon honey
- 1 teaspoon cinnamon
- 1/4 teaspoon nutmeg
- 4 slices whole meal bread, julienned

Directions:

1. In a suitable bowl, mix everything except the bread.
2. Dip each strip in the mixture. Place the bread strips on the Ninja Foodi basket.
3. Place basket inside the pot. Cover with the crisping lid. Select "Air Crisp" cooking mode.
4. Cook at 320 degrees F temperature for almost 10 minutes.
5. Serve warm.

Nutrition Values Per Serving:

Calories: 295, Total fat: 6.1g, Carbohydrates: 50g, Protein: 11.9g

Mustard Rubbed Pork Chops

Prep Time: 10 minutes

Cooking time: 30 minutes

Servings: 4

Ingredients:

- 2 tablespoons butter
- 2 tablespoons Dijon mustard
- 4 pork chops
- Salt and black pepper, to taste
- 1 tablespoon fresh rosemary, chopped

Directions:

1. Take a suitable bowl and add pork chops, cover with Dijon mustard, rosemary, salt, and pepper. Let it marinate for 2 hours
2. Add butter and marinated pork chops to your Ninja Foodi pot
3. Lock the Ninja Foodi's lid and cook on Low-Medium Pressure for 30 minutes
4. Release pressure naturally over 10 minutes.
5. Serve and enjoy!

Nutrition Values Per Serving:

Calories: 315, Total fat: 26g, Carbohydrates: 1g, Protein: 18g

Sweet Crepes

Prep Time: 5 minutes

Cooking time: 10 minutes

Servings: 4

Ingredients:

- 1 1/2 teaspoon Splenda
- 3 eggs
- 3 tablespoons coconut flour
- 1/2 cup heavy cream
- 3 tablespoons coconut oil, melted and divided

Directions:

1. Mix in 1 1/2 tablespoons coconut oil, Splenda, eggs, salt in a suitable bowl.
2. Add coconut flour and keep beating. Stir in heavy cream, beat well

3. Set your Ninja Foodi to Sauté mode and add 1/4 of the mixture
4. Sauté for 2 minutes on each side. Repeat until all ingredients are used.
5. Enjoy!

Nutrition Values Per Serving:

Calories: 145, Total fat: 13g, Carbohydrates: 4g, Protein: 4g

Garlicky Potatoes

Prep Time: 1 hour 10 minutes

Cooking time: 20 minutes

Servings: 2

Ingredients:

- 2 potatoes, scrubbed, rinsed and diced
- 1 tablespoon olive oil
- Salt to taste
- 1/4 teaspoon garlic powder

Directions:

1. Put the potatoes in a suitable bowl of cold water. Soak for 45 minutes.
2. Pat the potatoes dry with a paper towel. Toss in olive oil, salt and garlic powder.
3. Place in the Ninja Foodi basket. Seal the crisping lid. Select "Air Crisp" cooking mode.
4. Cook at 400 degrees F temperature for almost 20 minutes. Flip the potatoes when cooked halfway through.
5. Serve warm.

Nutrition Values Per Serving:

Calories: 208, Total fat: 7.2g, Carbohydrates: 34g, Protein: 3.6g

Seasoned Tofu Scramble

Prep Time: 30 minutes

Cooking time: 15 minutes

Servings: 4

Ingredients:

- 2 tablespoons olive oil, divided
- 2 tablespoons soy sauce
- 1/2 cup onion, chopped
- 1 teaspoon turmeric
- 1/2 teaspoon onion powder
- 1/2 teaspoon garlic powder
- 1 block firm tofu, sliced into cubes

Directions:

1. Mix all the ingredients except the tofu. Soak the tofu in the mixture.
2. Place the tofu in the Ninja Foodi pot. Seal the pot. Cover with the crisping lid.
3. Cook at 370 degrees F temperature for almost 15 minutes.
4. Serve warm.

Nutrition Values Per Serving:

Calories: 90, Total fat: 8g, Carbohydrates: 3.2g, Protein: 2.7g

Buffalo Wings

Prep Time: 10 minutes

Cooking time: 6 hours

Servings: 4

Ingredients:

- 1 bottle of (12 ounces) hot pepper sauce
- ½ cup melted ghee
- 1 tablespoon dried oregano
- 2 teaspoons garlic powder
- 1 teaspoon onion powder
- 5 pounds chicken wing sections

Directions:

1. Mix ghee, hot sauce, oregano, garlic powder, onion powder in a suitable bowl.
2. Add chicken wings and toss to coat.
3. Pour this mix into Ninja Foodi's insert and cook on "Slow Cook" mode with LOW heat for 6 hours.
4. Serve and enjoy!

Nutrition Values Per Serving:

Calories: 529, Total fat: 4g, Carbohydrates: 1g, Protein: 31g

Nutty Brussels Sprouts

Prep Time: 10 minutes

Cooking time: 3 minutes

Servings: 4

Ingredients:

- 1-pound Brussels sprouts
- ¼ cup pine nuts
- 1 tablespoon olive oil
- 1 pomegranate
- ½ teaspoon salt
- 1 pepper, grated

Directions:

1. Remove outer leaves and trim the stems off the washed Brussels sprouts
2. Cut the largest ones in uniform halves
3. Add 1 cup of water to the Ninja Foodi
4. Place steamer basket and add sprouts in the basket
5. Seal the lid and cook on "Pressure" mode at High for 3 minutes
6. Release the pressure naturally
7. Transfer the sprouts to the serving dish and dress with olive oil, pepper, and salt.

8. Sprinkle toasted pine nuts and pomegranate seeds!

9. Serve warm and enjoy!

Nutrition Values Per Serving:

Calories: 118, Total fat: 10g, Carbohydrates: 7g, Protein: 3g

Crispy Zucchini Fries

Prep Time: 10 minutes

Cooking time: 10 minutes

Servings: 4

Ingredients:

- 1-2 pounds of zucchini, sliced into 2 and ½ inch sticks
- Salt to taste
- 1 cup cream cheese
- 2 tablespoons olive oil

Directions:

1. Add zucchini in a colander and season with salt, add cream cheese and mix

2. Add oil into your Ninja Foodie's pot and add Zucchini.

3. Lock the Air Crisping Lid and set the temperature to 365 degrees F and timer to 10 minutes

4. Let it cook for 10 minutes and take the dish out once done, enjoy!

Nutrition Values Per Serving:

Calories: 374, Total fat: 36g, Carbohydrates: 6g, Protein: 7g

Bacon-Wrapped Drumsticks

Prep Time: 10 minutes

Cooking time: 8 hours

Servings: 6

Ingredients:

- 12 chicken drumsticks
- 12 slices thin-cut bacon

Directions:

1. Wrap each chicken drumsticks in bacon. Place drumsticks in your Ninja Foodi's insert.

2. Place lid and cook "Slow Cook" cooking mode with LOW heat for 8 hours.

3. Serve and enjoy!

Nutrition Values Per Serving:

Calories: 202, Total fat: 8g, Carbohydrates: 3g, Protein: 30g

Orange Cauliflower Salad

Prep Time: 10 minutes

Cooking time: 10 minutes

Servings: 4

Ingredients:

- 1 small-sized cauliflower, florets

- 1 Romanesco cauliflower, florets
- 1 pound of broccoli florets
- 2 seedless oranges, peeled and sliced

For vinaigrette

- 1 orange, juiced and zest
- 4 anchovies
- 1 hot pepper, sliced and chopped
- 1 tablespoon of capers
- 4 tablespoon of extra virgin olive oil
- Salt as needed
- Pepper as needed

Directions:

1. Add broccoli, cauliflower florets to your Ninja Foodi
2. Seal the lid and cook on "Pressure" mode at High for 7 minutes
3. Once done, quick-release the pressure and remove the lid.
4. Make the vinaigrette by mixing the hot pepper, anchovies, olive oil, capers, pepper, salt, and mix well.
5. Strain the veggies out and mix with vinaigrette and the orange slices.
6. Enjoy!

Nutrition Values Per Serving:

Calories: 163, Total fats: 11g, Carbs: 15g, Protein: 3g

Pickled Green Chili

Prep Time: 5 minutes

Cooking time: 11 minutes

Servings: 4

Ingredients:

- 1-pound green chilies
- 1 and ½ cups apple cider vinegar
- 1 teaspoon pickling salt
- 1 and ½ teaspoon sugar
- ¼ teaspoon garlic powder

Directions:

1. Add the green Chilli ingredients to the Ninja Foodi's pot.
2. Seal the lid and cook on "Pressure" mode at High for 11 minutes.
3. Release the pressure naturally
4. Spoon the mixture into jars and cover the slices with cooking liquid.
5. Refrigerate the chilies overnight.
6. Serve!

Nutrition Values Per Serving:

Calories: 3, Total fat: 0g, Carbohydrates: 0.8g, Protein: 0.1g

Chicken Stuffed Mushrooms

Prep Time: 10 minutes

Cooking time: 20 minutes

Servings: 4

Ingredients:

- 12 large fresh mushrooms, stems removed

Stuffing

- 1 cup chicken meat, cubed
- ½ pound, imitation crabmeat, flaked
- 2 cups butter
- Garlic powder to taste
- 2 garlic cloves, peeled and minced

Directions:

1. Take a suitable skillet and place it over medium heat, add butter and let it heat
2. Stir in meat chicken then sauté for 5 minutes.
3. Add rest of the ingredients for stuffing and cook for 5 minutes
4. Remove heat and let the chicken cool down. Divide filling into mushroom caps
5. Place stuffed mushroom caps in your Crisping basket and transfer basket to Foodi
6. Lock the Crisping Lid and cook on the "Air Crisp" mode for 10 minutes at 375 degrees F.
7. Serve and enjoy!

Nutrition Values Per Serving:

Calories: 385, Total fat: 36g, Carbohydrates: 4g, Protein: 8g

Zucchini Gratin

Prep Time: 10 minutes

Cooking time: 15 minutes

Servings: 4

Ingredients:

- 2 zucchinis
- 1 tablespoon fresh parsley, chopped
- 2 tablespoons bread crumbs
- 4 tablespoons parmesan cheese, grated
- 1 tablespoon vegetable oil
- Salt and black pepper, to taste

Directions:

1. Pre-heat your Ninja Foodi to 300 degrees F temperature for almost 3 minutes
2. Slice zucchini lengthwise to get about 8 equal sizes pieces
3. Arrange the zucchini pieces in the Crisping Basket, with your skin side down.
4. Top each with parsley, bread crumbs, cheese, oil, salt, and pepper
5. Return basket to the Ninja Foodi Air Fryer's insert and cook for 15 minutes at 360 degrees F.
6. Enjoy!

Nutrition Values Per Serving:

Calories: 481, Total fat: 11g, Carbohydrates: 10g, Protein: 7g

Cider dipped Chicken Thighs

Prep Time: 5 minutes

Cooking time: 6-8 hours

Servings: 6

Ingredients:

- 3 pounds boneless chicken thighs, skinless
- 2 tablespoons apple cider vinegar
- ½ cup agave nectar
- 2 teaspoon garlic powder
- 2 teaspoons paprika
- 1 teaspoon Chilli powder
- 1 teaspoon red pepper flakes
- 1 teaspoon black pepper
- 2 teaspoon salt

Directions:

1. Mix paprika, red pepper flakes, Chilli powder, garlic pepper, salt, and pepper in a bowl.
2. Take another bowl and mix vinegar and agave nectar.
3. Use the seasoning mix to properly coat the chicken thigh.
4. Pour nectar, vinegar mix over chicken. Transfer the mix to Ninja Foodi
5. Lock the Ninja Foodi's lid and cook on "Slow Cook" cooking mode with low heat for 6-8 hours
6. Once done, unlock the lid. Drizzle the glaze on top and serve.
7. Enjoy!

Nutrition Values Per Serving:

Calories: 234, Total fat: 15g, Carbohydrates: 14g, Protein: 8g

Cheesy Chicken Parmesan

Prep Time: 10 minutes

Cooking time: 20 minutes

Servings: 4

Ingredients:

- 1 spaghetti squash
- 1 cup marinara sauce
- 1-pound chicken, cooked and cubed
- 16 ounces mozzarella

Directions:

1. Split the squash in halves and remove the seeds
2. Add 1 cup of water to the Ninja Foodi and place a trivet on top
3. Add the squash halves on the trivet. Seal the Ninja's lid and cook for 20 minutes at HIGH pressure
4. Do a quick release. Remove the squashes and shred them using a fork into spaghetti portions

5. Pour sauce over the squash and give it a nice mix
6. Top them with the cubed chicken and top with mozzarella
7. Broil for 1-2 minutes and broil until the cheese has melted.
8. Serve warm.

Nutrition Values Per Serving:

Calories: 127, Total fats: 8g, Carbs:11g, Protein:5g

Cider Dipped Chili

Prep Time: 10 minutes

Cooking time: 11 minutes

Servings: 4

Ingredients:

- 1-pound green chilies
- 1 and ½ cups apple cider vinegar
- 1 teaspoon pickling salt
- 1 and ½ teaspoons date paste
- ¼ teaspoon garlic powder

Directions:

1. Add the above-mentioned ingredients to the Ninja Foodi's insert.
2. Seal the lid and cook on "Pressure" mode at High for 10 minutes
3. Release the pressure naturally
4. Spoon the mix into washed jars and cover the slices with a bit of cooking liquid
5. Add vinegar to submerge the chilly.
6. Enjoy!

Nutrition Values Per Serving:

Calories: 3.1, Total fat: 0g, Carbohydrates: 0.6g, Protein: 0.1g

Crispy Beet Chips

Prep Time: 10 minutes

Cooking time: 8 hours

Servings: 8

Ingredients:

- ½ beet, peeled and sliced

Directions:

1. Arrange beet slices in a single layer in the Crisper basket of Ninja Foodi.
2. Place the basket into the Ninja Foodi's pot and close the crisping lid.
3. Press the Dehydrate button and let it dehydrate for 8 hours at 135 degrees F.
4. Once the dehydrating is done, remove the basket from the pot.
5. Serve.

Nutrition Values Per Serving:

Calories: 35, Total fat: 0g, Carbohydrates: 8g, Protein: 1g

Cheesy Mushroom Appetizer

Prep Time: 10 minutes

Cooking time: 20 minutes

Servings: 6

Ingredients:

- 24 mushrooms, caps and stems diced
- 1 cup cheddar cheese, shredded
- ½ orange bell pepper, diced
- ½ onion, diced
- 4 bacon slices, diced
- ½ cup sour cream

Directions:

1. Set your Ninja Foodie to Sauté mode and add mushroom stems, onion, bacon, bell pepper and Sauté for 5 minutes.
2. Add 1 cup cheese, sour cream and cook for 2 minutes.
3. Stuff mushrooms with cheese and vegetable mixture and top with cheddar cheese
4. Transfer them to your Crisping Basket and lock the Air Crisping lid.
5. Cook on "Air Crisp" mode for 8 minutes at 350 degrees F.
6. Serve and enjoy!

Nutrition Values Per Serving:

Calories: 288, Total fat: 6g, Carbohydrates: 3g, Protein: 25g

Saucy Chicken Thighs

Prep Time: 10 minutes

Cooking time: 5-7 hours

Servings: 4

Ingredients:

- 3 pounds boneless, skinless chicken thighs
- ½ cup low-sodium chicken broth
- 2 cups cherry tomatoes, halved
- 4 garlic cloves, minced
- 2 teaspoons garlic salt
- ¼ teaspoon ground white pepper
- 2 tablespoons fresh basil, chopped
- 2 tablespoons fresh oregano, chopped

Directions:

1. Add the chicken and all the listed ingredients to your Ninja Foodi and mix gently.
2. Lock the Ninja Foodi's lid and cook on "Slow Cook" mode with Low Heat for 5-7 hours.
3. Serve and enjoy!

Nutrition Values Per Serving:

Calories: 247, Total fat: 5g, Carbohydrates: 15g, Protein: 34g

Creamy Fudge Meal

Prep Time: 10 minutes + chill times

Cooking time: 10-20 minutes

Servings: 20

Ingredients:

- ½ teaspoon organic vanilla extract

- 1 cup heavy whip cream
- 2 ounces butter, soft
- 2 ounces 70% dark chocolate, finely chopped

Directions:

1. Set your Ninja Foodi to Sauté mode and add vanilla, heavy cream. Sauté for 5 minutes
2. Add butter and chocolate and Sauté for 2 minutes. Transfer to serving the dish
3. Chill for few hours and enjoy!

Nutrition Values Per Serving:

Calories: 292, Total fat: 26g, Carbohydrates: 8g, Protein: 5g

Bacon with Bok Choy

Prep Time: 10 minutes

Cooking time: 3 minutes

Servings: 4

Ingredients:

- ½ tablespoons fresh lemon juice
- 1 medium ripe avocado, peeled and pitted, chopped
- 6 organic eggs, boiled, peeled and cut half
- Salt to taste
- ½ cup fresh watercress, trimmed

Directions:

1. Place the Ninja's steamer basket at the bottom of the Ninja Foodi's insert.
2. Add water to the insert and put the watercress in the basket.
3. Lock the Ninja Foodi's lid and pressure cook for 3 minutes
4. Quick-release pressure, then remove the lid.
5. Allow the boiled eggs to cool, peel and cut them in half.
6. Remove egg yolk and transfer to a suitable bowl
7. Add watercress, avocado, lemon juice, salt, and mash well
8. Place egg whites in serving the dish and fill whites with watercress, mix well.
9. Enjoy!

Nutrition Values Per Serving:

Calories: 132, Total fat: 10g, Carbohydrates: 3g, Protein: 6g

Mexican Cheese Frittata

Prep Time: 10 minutes

Cooking time: 25 minutes

Servings: 4

Ingredients:

- 4 whole eggs
- 1 cup half and half
- 10 ounces canned green chilies

- ½ -1 teaspoon salt
- ½ teaspoon ground cumin
- 1 cup Mexican blend shredded cheese
- ¼ cup cilantro, chopped

Directions:

1. Take a suitable bowl and beat eggs and a half and half
2. Add diced green chilis, salt, cumin and ½ cup of shredded cheese
3. Pour the mixture into 6 inches greased metal pan and cover with foil
4. Add 2 cups of water to the Ninja Foodi.
5. Place trivet into the Ninja Foodi's pot and place the pan in the trivet
6. Seal the lid and cook on "Pressure" mode at High for 20 minutes
7. Release the pressure naturally over 10 minutes
8. Scatter half a cup of the cheese on top of your quiche.
9. Enjoy!

Nutrition Values Per Serving:

Calories: 257, Total fat: 19g, Carbohydrates: 6g, Protein:14g

Braised Kale Salad

Prep Time: 5 minutes

Cooking time: 8 minutes

Servings: 4

Ingredients:

- 10 ounces kale, chopped
- 1 tablespoon ghee
- 1 medium onion, sliced
- 3 medium carrots, cut into half-inch pieces
- 5 garlic cloves, peeled and chopped
- ½ cup chicken broth
- Fresh ground pepper
- Vinegar as needed
- ½ teaspoon red pepper flakes

Directions:

1. Set your pot to Sauté mode and add ghee, allow the ghee to melt
2. Add chopped onion and carrots and Sauté for a while
3. Add garlic and Sauté for a while. Pile the kale on top
4. Pour chicken broth and season with pepper
5. Seal the lid and cook on "Pressure" mode at High for 8 minutes
6. Release the pressure naturally over 10 minutes and remove the lid.
7. Add vinegar and sprinkle a bit more pepper flakes.
8. Enjoy!

Nutrition Values Per Serving:

Calories: 41, Total fat: 2g, Carbohydrates: 5g, Protein: 2g

Chapter 3-Pork, Beef & Lamb Recipes

Beef Jerky

Prep Time: 10 minutes

Cooking Time: 4 hours

Servings: 4

Ingredients:

- ½ pound beef, julienned
- 2 tablespoons Worcestershire sauce
- 1 teaspoon onion powder
- 1/2 cup of soy sauce
- 1/2 teaspoon garlic powder
- 1 teaspoon salt
- 2 teaspoons black pepper

Directions:

1. Take a large-sized Ziplock bag and add all the ingredients.
2. Seal and refrigerate the beef strips overnight.
3. Place the strips on a dehydrator tray and place them in the Ninja Foodi's pot.
4. Cook for 4 hours at 135-degree F on Dehydrate Mode.
5. Serve and enjoy!

Nutrition Values Per Serving:

Calories: 62, Total fat: 7g, Carbohydrates: 2g, Protein: 31g

Mexican Beef Short Ribs

Prep Time: 10 minutes

Cooking Time: 35 minutes

Servings: 4

Ingredients:

- 2 and ½ pounds boneless beef short ribs
- 1 tablespoon Chilli powder
- 1 and ½ teaspoons salt
- 1 tablespoon fat
- 1 medium onion, thinly sliced
- 1 tablespoon tomato sauce
- 6 garlic cloves, peeled and smashed
- ½ cup roasted tomato salsa
- ½ cup bone broth
- Fresh black pepper
- ½ cup cilantro, minced
- 2 radishes, sliced

Directions:

1. Mix beef, salt, Chilli powder in a suitable bowl.
2. Set the Ninja Foodi to Sauté mode, add butter to melt.
3. Add garlic, tomato paste, then sauté for 30 seconds
4. Add beef stock and fish sauce on top.
5. Lock the Ninja Foodi's lid and cook on "Pressure" mode on HIGH for 35 minutes.
6. Naturally, release pressure, then remove the lid.
7. Enjoy!

Nutrition Values Per Serving:

Calories: 308, Total fat: 18g, Carbohydrates: 21g, Protein: 38g

Adobo Beef Steak

Prep Time: 5 minutes

Cooking Time: 25 minutes

Servings: 4

Ingredients:

- 2 cups of water
- 8 steaks, cubed, 28 ounces pack
- Black pepper to taste
- 1 and ¾ teaspoons adobo seasoning
- 1 can (8 ounces) tomato sauce
- 1/3 cup green pitted olives
- 2 tablespoons brine
- 1 small red pepper
- 1/2 a medium onion, sliced

Directions:

1. Chop onions and peppers into 1/4-inch strips
2. Season the beef with pepper and adobo.
3. Add to the Ninja Foodi's insert, then add remaining ingredients and Close the Ninja's lid.
4. Cook on "Pressure" mode for 25 minutes on HIGH.
5. Release pressure naturally, then remove the lid.
6. Serve and enjoy!

Nutrition Values Per Serving:

Calories: 429, Total fat: 24g, Carbohydrates: 11g, Protein: 31g

Tomato Beef Stew

Prep Time: 11 minutes

Cooking Time: 10 minutes

Servings: 4

Ingredients:

- 1-pound beef roast
- 4 cups beef broth
- 2 tomatoes, chopped
- 1/2 white onion, chopped
- 3 garlic cloves, chopped

- 1 carrot, chopped
- 2 celery stalks, chopped
- 1/4 teaspoon salt
- 1/8 teaspoon black pepper

Directions:

1. Add beef roast along with all ingredients to your Ninja Foodi's inset.
2. Cover the Foodi's lid and seal it for pressure cooking.
3. Cook on "Pressure" mode for 10 minutes on HIGH.
4. Release pressure naturally, then remove the lid.
5. Serve and enjoy!

Nutrition Values Per Serving:

Calories: 529, Total fat: 4g, Carbohydrates: 1g, Protein: 31g

Smothered Pork Chops

Prep Time: 10 minutes

Cooking Time: 28 minutes

Servings: 4

Ingredients:

- 6 ounce of boneless pork loin chops
- 1 tablespoon of paprika
- 1 teaspoon of garlic powder
- 1 teaspoon of onion powder
- 1 teaspoon of black pepper
- 1 teaspoon of salt
- 1/4 teaspoon of cayenne pepper
- 2 tablespoon of coconut oil
- 1/2 of a sliced medium onion
- 6-ounce baby Bella mushrooms, sliced
- 1 tablespoon of butter
- 1/2 a cup of whip cream
- 1/4 teaspoon of xanthan gum
- 1 tablespoon parsley, chopped

Directions:

1. Mix garlic powder, paprika, onion powder, black pepper, salt, and cayenne pepper
2. Rub the seasoning all over the meat
3. Reserve the remaining spice mixture
4. Set your Ninja Foodi to Sauté mode and add coconut oil to heat.
5. Brown the chops 3 minutes per sides.
6. Add sliced onion to the base of your Ninja Foodi along with mushrooms.
7. Top with the browned pork chops, then seal the lid to cook for 10 minutes on High pressure.
8. Release the pressure and remove the lid. Transfer the pork chops to a plate.

9. Set your Ninja Foodi to Sauté mode and whisk in remaining spices mix, heavy cream, and butter
10. Sprinkle 1/4 teaspoon of xanthan gum and stir
11. Simmer for 3-5 minutes and remove the heat
12. Serve warm with the pork.

Nutrition Values Per Serving:

Calories: 481, Total fat: 32g, Carbohydrates: 6g, Protein: 39g

Beef Pork Chili

Prep Time: 10 minutes

Cooking Time: 35 minutes

Servings: 4

Ingredients:

- 1-pound ground beef
- 1-pound ground pork
- 3 tomatillos, chopped
- 1 teaspoon garlic powder
- 1 jalapeno pepper
- 1 tablespoon ground cumin
- 1 tablespoon Chilli powder
- Salt as needed

Directions:

1. Set your Ninja Foodi to Sauté mode and add beef and pork. Sauté until brown.
2. Add onion, garlic, tomatillo, tomato paste, jalapeno, cumin, water, Chilli powder, and mix well.
3. Seal the lid and cook on "Pressure" mode on High for 35 minutes.
4. Release the Pressure naturally, then remove the lid.
5. Serve and enjoy!

Nutrition Values Per Serving:

Calories: 325, Total fat: 23g, Carbohydrates: 6g, Protein: 20g

Kale Sausage Soup

Prep Time: 5-10 minutes

Cooking Time: 10 minutes

Servings: 4

Ingredients:

- 1/2 diced onion
- 2 cup chicken broth
- 1-pound chopped sausage roll
- 1 tablespoon olive oil
- 2 cup almond milk
- 1/2 cup parmesan cheese
- 3 cup chopped kale fresh

- 28-ounce tomatoes, crushed
- 1 tablespoon minced garlic
- 1 teaspoon oregano, dried
- 1/4 teaspoon salt

Directions:

1. Preheat your Ninja Foodi on "SEAR/SAUTÉ" mode.
2. Add the sausage and stir-cook to brown evenly.
3. Stir in spices, onions, kale, tomatoes, milk, and chicken broth, then mix well.
4. Select "PRESSURE" mode with high pressure level and seal the lid.
5. Naturally, release inside pressure for about 8-10 minutes.
6. Serve warm with the cheese on top.
7. Enjoy.

Nutrition Values Per Serving:

Calories: 162, Total fat: 11g, Carbohydrates: 2g, Protein: 19g

Jamaican Pork Meal

Prep Time: 10 minutes

Cooking Time: 30 minutes

Servings: 4

Ingredients:

- 1/2 cup beef stock
- 1 tablespoon olive oil
- 1/4 cup Jamaican jerk spice blend
- 4 ounces of pork shoulder

Directions:

1. Rub roast with olive oil and spice blend
2. Set your Ninja Foodi to Sauté mode and add meat, brown all sides
3. Pour beef broth and seal the lid.
4. Cook on "Pressure" cook mode at High for 30 minutes.
5. Release the pressure completely then remove the lid and shred the meat.
6. Serve warm.

Nutrition Values Per Serving:

Calories: 308, Total fat: 18g, Carbohydrates: 5g, Protein: 31g

Mustard Glazed Pork

Prep Time: 10 minutes

Cooking Time: 30 minutes

Servings: 4

Ingredients:

- 2 tablespoons ghee
- 2 tablespoons Dijon mustard

- 4 pork chops
- Salt and black pepper, to taste
- 1 tablespoon fresh rosemary, chopped

Directions:

1. Take a suitable bowl and add pork chops, cover with Dijon mustard and carefully sprinkle rosemary, salt, and pepper
2. Let it marinate for 2 hours
3. Add ghee and marinated pork chops to your Ninja Foodi pot
4. Lock the Ninja Foodi's lid and cook on Low-Medium Pressure for 30 minutes
5. Release pressure naturally over 10 minutes
6. Serve and enjoy.

Nutrition Values Per Serving:

Calories: 315, Total fat: 26g, Carbohydrates: 1g, Protein: 18g

Onion Pork Chops

Prep Time: 10 minutes

Cooking Time: 20 minutes

Servings: 4

Ingredients:

- 4 pork chops
- 10 ounces French Onion Soup
- ½ cup sour cream
- 10 ounces chicken broth

Directions:

1. Add pork chops and broth to your Ninja Foodi's insert.
2. Lock the Ninja Foodi's lid and cook on "Pressure" mode at High for 12 minutes
3. Release pressure naturally over 10 minutes, then remove the lid.
4. Whisk sour cream and French Onion Soup and pour mixture over pork
5. Set your Ninja Foodi to Sauté mode and cook for 6-8 minutes more
6. Serve and enjoy!

Nutrition Values Per Serving:

Calories: 356, Total fat: 26g, Carbohydrates: 7g, Protein: 21g

Ranch Beef Roast

Prep Time: 10 minutes

Cooking Time: 60 minutes

Servings: 4

Ingredients:

- 3 pounds beef roast
- 1 tablespoon olive oil
- 2 tablespoons ranch dressing

- 1 jar pepper rings, with juices
- 8 tablespoons butter
- 1 cup of water

Directions:

1. Set your Ninja Foodi to Sauté mode and add 1 tablespoon of oil
2. Once the oil is hot, add roast and sear on both sides.
3. Add water, reserved juice, seasoning mix, and pepper rings on top of the beef.
4. Seal the lid and cook on "Pressure" mode on HIGH for 60 minutes.
5. Release the pressure naturally over 10 minutes
6. Cut the beef with salad sheers and enjoy with pureed cauliflower
7. Enjoy!

Nutrition Values Per Serving:

Calories: 365, Total fat: 18g, Carbohydrates: 12g, Protein: 16g

Indian Beef Meal

Prep Time: 10 minutes

Cooking Time: 20 minutes

Servings: 4

Ingredients:

- ½ yellow onion, chopped
- 1 tablespoon olive oil
- 2 garlic cloves, minced
- 1 jalapeno pepper, chopped
- 1 cup cherry tomatoes, quartered
- 1 teaspoon fresh lemon juice
- 1-2 pounds grass-fed ground beef
- 1-2 pounds fresh collard greens, trimmed and chopped

Spices

- 1 teaspoon cumin, ground
- ½ teaspoon ginger, ground
- 1 teaspoon coriander, ground
- ½ teaspoon fennel seeds, ground
- ½ teaspoon cinnamon, ground
- Salt and black pepper, to taste
- ½ teaspoon turmeric, ground

Directions:

1. Set your Ninja Foodi to Sauté mode, add garlic and onion, then Sauté for 3 minutes.
2. Add Jalapeno pepper, beef, spices and stir well.
3. Lock the Ninja Foodi's lid and cook on "Pressure" mode on MEDIUM for 15 minutes.
4. Release pressure naturally and remove the lid.
5. Add tomatoes and collard, sauté for 3 minutes

6. Stir in lemon juice, salt, and black pepper, then mix well.

7. Serve and enjoy!

Nutrition Values Per Serving:

Calories: 409, Total fat: 16g, Carbohydrates: 5g, Protein: 56g

New York Steak

Prep Time: 10 minutes

Cooking Time: 9 minutes

Servings: 4

Ingredients:

- 24 ounces NY strip steak
- ½ teaspoon black pepper
- 1 teaspoon salt

Directions:

1. Add steaks on a metal trivet, place it on your Ninja Foodi

2. For seasoning, add salt and black pepper on top.

3. Add 1 cup water to the Ninja Foodi's pot.

4. Cover the Foodi's lid and seal it for pressure cooking.

5. Cook on "Pressure" mode for 1 minute on HIGH.

6. Release pressure naturally, then remove the lid.

7. Place Air-crisp lid and cook on the "Air Crisp" mode for 8 minutes for a medium-steak.

8. Serve and enjoy!

Nutrition Values Per Serving:

Calories: 503, Total fat: 46g, Carbohydrates: 1g, Protein: 46g

Cheesy Beef Meatloaf

Prep Time: 5-10 minutes

Cooking Time: 70 minutes

Servings: 6

Ingredients:

- 1/4 cup tomato puree or crushed tomatoes
- 1-pound lean ground beef
- 1/2 cup onion, chopped
- 2 garlic cloves, minced
- 1/2 cup green bell pepper, chopped
- 2 eggs, beaten
- 1 cup cheddar cheese, grated
- 3 cups spinach, chopped
- 1 teaspoon dried thyme, crushed
- 6 cups mozzarella cheese, grated
- Black pepper to taste

Directions:

1. Grease a baking pan with cooking spray.

2. Mix all the listed ingredients except cheese and spinach.

3. Place the prepared mixture over the wax paper; top it with spinach, cheese, and roll it to make a meatloaf.

4. Remove wax paper and add the rolled meatloaf to the baking pan.

5. Add water to the Ninja Foodi's pot and place a reversible rack inside the pot.

6. Place the pan on the rack.

7. Select "BAKE/ROAST" mode and adjust the 380 degrees F temperature.

8. Then, set the timer to 70 minutes and hit "STOP/START."

9. Serve warm.

Nutrition Values Per Serving:

Calories: 426, Total fat: 17g, Carbohydrates: 5.5g, Protein: 49g

Lemon Pork Cutlets

Prep Time: 10 minutes

Cooking Time: 5 minutes

Servings: 4

Ingredients:

- ½ cup hot sauce
- ½ cup of water
- 2 tablespoons butter
- 1/3 cup lemon juice
- 1-pound pork cutlets
- ½ teaspoon paprika

Directions:

1. Add pork cutlets and all other listed ingredients to the Ninja Foodi.

2. Lock the Ninja Foodi's lid and cook on "Pressure" mode at High for 5 minutes.

3. Now release the cooker's pressure naturally for 10 minutes, then remove the lid.

4. Gently mix and serve warm.

Nutrition Values Per Serving:

Calories: 414, Total fat: 21g, Carbohydrates: 3g, Protein: 50g

Beef Meatballs with Marinara Sauce

Prep Time: 10 minutes

Cooking Time: 11 minutes

Servings: 4

Ingredients:

- 2 cups ground beef
- 1 egg, beaten
- 1 teaspoon taco seasoning
- 1 tablespoon sugar-free marinara sauce
- 1 teaspoon garlic, minced
- ½ teaspoon salt

Directions:

1. Mix ground beef with egg, taco seasoning and the rest of the ingredients in a bowl.

2. Make golf-ball sized meatballs out of this mixture and put them in a single layer in the Air fryer's Basket.

3. Cover the crisping lid and cook on "Air Crisp" mode for 11 minutes at 350 degrees F.

4. Serve immediately and enjoy!

Nutrition Values Per Serving:

Calories: 205, Total fat: 12g, Carbohydrates: 2g, Protein: 19g

Saucy Lamb Roast

Prep Time: 10 minutes

Cooking Time: 60 minutes

Servings: 4

Ingredients:

- 2 pounds lamb roasted Wegmans
- 1 cup beef broth
- 1 cup onion soup
- Salt and black pepper, to taste

Directions:

1. Place your lamb roast in your Ninja Foodi pot
2. Add beef broth, onion soup, salt and black pepper.
3. Cover the Foodi's lid and seal it for pressure cooking.
4. Cook on "Pressure" mode for 55 minutes on HIGH.
5. Release pressure naturally, then remove the lid.
6. Serve and enjoy!

Nutrition Values Per Serving:

Calories: 211, Total fat: 7g, Carbohydrates: 2g, Protein: 30g

Herbed Pork Chops

Prep Time: 10 minutes

Cooking Time: 30 minutes

Servings: 4

Ingredients:

- 2 tablespoons ghee
- 2 tablespoons Dijon mustard
- 4 pork chops
- Salt and black pepper, to taste
- 1 tablespoon fresh rosemary, chopped

Directions:

1. Take a suitable bowl and add pork chops, cover with Dijon mustard and carefully sprinkle rosemary, salt, and black pepper.
2. Let it marinate for 2 hours
3. Add ghee and marinated pork chops to your Ninja Foodi pot.
4. Cover the Foodi's lid and seal it for pressure cooking.
5. Cook on "Pressure" mode for 30 minutes on Low.
6. Release pressure naturally, then remove the lid.
7. Serve and enjoy!

Nutrition Values Per Serving:

Calories: 315, Total fat: 26g, Carbohydrates: 1g, Protein: 18g

Chicken Cauliflower Pilaf

Prep Time: 15 minutes

Cooking time: 6 minutes

Servings: 10

Ingredients:

- 1 cup cauliflower rice
- 7 ounces chicken breasts, boneless
- 1 teaspoon salt
- 4 ounces mushrooms
- 1 tablespoon olive oil
- 1 white onion
- 1 tablespoon oregano
- 4 ounces raisins
- 5 ounces kale
- 7 ounces green beans
- 3 cups chicken stock
- 2 tablespoons oyster sauce

Directions:

1. Slice the mushrooms and place them into the Ninja Foodi.
2. Chop the chicken breasts into medium-sized pieces and add them to the Ninja Foodi.
3. Peel the onion and dice it. Chop the kale and green beans.
4. Transfer the vegetables to the Ninja Foodi.
5. Top the mixture with olive oil, salt, oregano, raisins, and chicken stock.
6. Set the Ninja Foodi to" Pressure" mode and stir well.
7. Add the cauliflower rice and close the Ninja Foodi's lid.
8. Cook on "Pressure" mode for 6 minutes at High.
9. Once it is done, release the cooker's pressure then remove the Ninja Foodi's lid.
10. Let the pilaf rest and stir well before serving.

Nutrition Values Per Serving:

Calories: 111, Total fat: 3.2g, Fiber: 2.1g, Carbohydrates: 14.4g, Protein: 7.8g

Coconut Dipped Chicken Strips

Prep Time: 10 minutes

Cooking time: 12 minutes

Servings: 8

Ingredients:

- ½ cup coconut
- 4 tablespoons butter

- 1 teaspoon salt
- ⅓ cup flour
- ½ teaspoon Sugar
- ¼ teaspoon red Chilli flakes
- 1 teaspoon onion powder
- 15 ounces boneless chicken breast

Directions:

1. Cut the boneless chicken breast into the strips, sprinkle it with the salt and Chilli flakes, and stir.

2. Mix the coconut, flour, sugar, and onion powder in a suitable mixing bowl and stir well.

3. Set the Ninja Foodi to" Sauté" mode.

4. Add the butter into the Ninja Foodi and cook for 2 minutes.

5. Dip the chicken strips in the coconut mixture well and transfer the chicken strips into the Ninja Foodi.

6. Sauté the dish for 10 minutes on both sides.

7. When the chicken is golden brown, remove the chicken strips to a plate.

8. Let the dish rest briefly and serve.

Nutrition Values Per Serving:

Calories: 197, Total fat: 13.7g, Fiber: 1g, Carbohydrates: 2.3g, Protein: 16.6g

Seasoned Whole Chicken

Prep Time: 15 minutes

Cooking time: 30 minutes

Servings: 9

Ingredients:

- 2 pounds whole chicken, wash and cleaned
- 1 tablespoon salt
- 1 teaspoon black pepper
- 1 tablespoon olive oil
- 1 teaspoon butter
- 1 teaspoon fresh rosemary
- 1 lemon
- 1 tablespoon sugar
- 1 cup of water
- 1 teaspoon coriander, chopped
- ½ teaspoon cayenne pepper
- ¼ teaspoon turmeric

Directions:

1. Mix the salt, black pepper, fresh rosemary, sugar, coriander, cayenne pepper, and turmeric in a suitable mixing bowl.

2. Rub the chicken with the spice mixture.

3. Sprinkle the chicken with olive oil. Set the Ninja Foodi to" Pressure" mode.

4. Pour the water into the Ninja Foodi and place the stuffed whole chicken.

5. Seal the lid and cook for 30 minutes at HI pressure.

6. Once it is done, release the cooker's pressure and open the Ninja Foodi's lid.

7. Remove the prepared chicken from the Ninja Foodi and let it rest.

8. Cut the cooked chicken into pieces and serve warm.

Nutrition Values Per Serving:

Calories: 217, Total fat: 9.5g, Fiber: 0.3g, Carbohydrates: 2.3g, Protein: 29.3g

Mexican Chicken with Salsa

Prep Time: 13 minutes

Cooking time: 15 minutes

Servings: 6

Ingredients:

- 1 cup of salsa
- 1 teaspoon paprika
- 1 teaspoon salt
- 2 tablespoons minced garlic
- 15 ounces boneless chicken breast
- 1 teaspoon oregano

Directions:

1. Mix the paprika, salt, minced garlic, and oregano in a suitable mixing bowl and stir.

2. Chop the boneless chicken breast and sprinkle it with the spice mixture.

3. Set the Ninja Foodi to" Pressure" mode.

4. Transfer the chicken mixture into the Ninja Foodi, add the salsa, and mix well using a wooden spoon.

5. Close the Ninja's lid and cook for 15 minutes.

6. Once it is done, release the cooker's pressure and open the Ninja Foodi's lid.

7. Transfer the cooked chicken with salsa to a serving bowl.

Nutrition Values Per Serving:

Calories: 206, Total fat: 10.3g, Fiber: 3g, Carbohydrates: 20.49g, Protein: 9g

Chicken Mushrooms Rice

Prep Time: 15 minutes

Cooking time: 35 minutes

Servings: 8

Ingredients:

- 1 cup cauliflower rice
- 3 cups chicken stock
- 1 tablespoon salt
- 2 tablespoons butter
- 2 big carrots, peeled and chopped
- 1 white onion, chopped
- 8 ounces mushrooms, chopped
- 1 tablespoon dry dill
- 1 tablespoon cream
- 1 teaspoon rosemary

- 1 teaspoon ground cumin
- 1 teaspoon paprika
- 1 teaspoon oregano
- 1 tablespoon cilantro, chopped
- 1 teaspoon chives, chopped
- 1-pound chicken breast, diced

Directions:

1. Mix the rosemary, cream, black pepper, oregano, paprika, cilantro, and chives in a suitable mixing bowl.

2. Add chopped chicken breast to the cream mixture and mix well.

3. Set the Ninja Foodi to" Sauté" mode. Stir in butter to melt.

4. Add the sliced vegetables and sauté for 10 minutes.

5. Add the creamy chicken mixture, chicken stock, and cauliflower rice.

6. Close the Ninja's lid and cook on" Manual" mode for 25 minutes.

7. Once done, remove the lid and serve warm.

Nutrition Values Per Serving:

Calories: 121, Total fat: 4.8g, Fiber: 1.6g, Carbohydrates: 5.7g, Protein: 14g

Creamy Pulled Chicken

Prep Time: 15 minutes

Cooking time: 25 minutes

Servings: 7

Ingredients:

- 1 cup cream
- 1 cup chicken stock
- 1 tablespoon garlic sauce
- 1 tablespoon minced garlic
- 1 teaspoon nutmeg
- 1 teaspoon salt
- 12 ounces of chicken breasts
- 1 tablespoon lemon juice

Directions:

1. Mix the nutmeg and salt and stir well.

2. Sprinkle the chicken breasts with the salt mixture, coating them well.

3. Set the Ninja Foodi to" Pressure" mode.

4. Place the chicken into the Ninja Foodi.

5. Add chicken stock, minced garlic, and cream, stir well and Close the Ninja's lid.

6. Cook on "Pressure" mode at High for 25 minutes.

7. Once it is done, release the cooker's pressure and open the Ninja Foodi's lid.

8. Transfer the chicken to a mixing bowl.

9. Shred the meat using a fork. Add the garlic sauce, mix well, and serve.

Nutrition Values Per Serving:

Calories: 169, Total fat: 11.8g, Fiber: 0g, Carbohydrates: 3.32g, Protein: 12g

Chicken Noodle Soup

Prep Time: 15 minutes

Cooking time: 29 minutes

Servings: 9

Ingredients:

- 6 ounces Shirataki noodles
- 8 cups of water
- 1 carrot
- 1 tablespoon peanut oil
- 1 yellow onion
- ½ tablespoon salt
- 3 ounces celery stalk
- 1 teaspoon black pepper
- ½ lemon
- 1 teaspoon minced garlic
- 10 ounces chicken breast

Directions:

1. Peel the carrot and onion and dice them.
2. Cut the chicken breast into halves.
3. Set the Ninja Foodi to" Pressure" mode.
4. Pour the peanut oil into the Ninja Foodi and preheat it for 1 minute.
5. Add the onion and carrot and stir well; cook it for 5 minutes, stirring constantly.
6. Add 4 cups of water and chicken breast.
7. Close the Ninja's lid and cook the dish on" Pressure" mode for 10 minutes.
8. Once it is done, remove the chicken from the Ninja Foodi and shred it.
9. Return the shredded chicken to the Ninja Foodi and Close the Ninja's lid.
10. Cook the dish for 7 minutes. Add 4 cups of water and Shirataki noodles.
11. Close the Ninja's lid and cook the dish on "Pressure" mode for 7 minutes.
12. When the soup is done, transfer it from the Ninja Foodi to the serving bowls.

Nutrition Values Per Serving:

Calories: 64, Total fat: 2.3g, Fiber: 2.7g, Carbohydrates: 2.6g, Protein: 7.2g

Italian Chicken Breasts

Prep Time: 10 minutes

Cooking time: 25 minutes

Servings: 6

Ingredients:

- 13-ounce Italian-style salad dressing
- 1 teaspoon butter
- 1-pound chicken breast, skinless

Directions:

1. Chop the chicken breasts roughly and place them in a suitable mixing bowl.
2. Sprinkle the chopped meat with the Italian-style salad dressing and mix well using your hands.
3. Let the chicken marinate breast for 1 hour in your refrigerator.
4. Set the Ninja Foodi to" Pressure" mode.
5. Add the butter into the Ninja Foodi.
6. Add marinated chicken breast and cook for 25 minutes.
7. Once it is done, remove the chicken from the Ninja Foodi and let it rest briefly.
8. Transfer the dish to a serving plate.

Nutrition Values Per Serving:

Calories: 283, Total fat: 20.6g, Fiber: 0g, Carbohydrates: 7.45g, Protein: 16g

Chicken Thigh Puttanesca

Prep Time: 15 minutes

Cooking time: 25 minutes

Servings: 8

Ingredients:

- 1 ½ pounds chicken thighs
- ½ cup tomato paste
- 2 tablespoons capers
- 1 teaspoon salt
- 1/2 teaspoons black-eyed peas
- 3 garlic cloves
- 3 tablespoons olive oil
- 4 ounces black olives
- 1 tablespoon fresh basil, chopped
- ½ cup of water

Directions:

1. Set the Ninja Foodi to" Sauté" mode.
2. Pour the olive oil into the Ninja Foodi and preheat it for 1 minute.
3. Place the chicken thighs into the Ninja Foodi and sauté the chicken for 5 minutes.
4. Once the chicken thighs are golden, remove them from the Ninja Foodi and keep aside.
5. Put the tomato paste, capers, olives, black-eyed peas, and basil into the Ninja Foodi.
6. Peel the garlic and slice it. Add the sliced garlic to the Ninja Foodi mixture.
7. Add the salt and water. Stir the mixture well and sauté it for 3 minutes.
8. Add the chicken thighs and Close the Ninja's lid.
9. Cook the dish on" Pressure" mode for 17 minutes.
10. Once it is done, open the Ninja Foodi's lid and transfer the dish to the serving bowl.

Nutrition Values Per Serving:

Calories: 170, Total fat: 8.8g, Fiber: 1g, Carbohydrates: 4.48g, Protein: 18g

Creamy Stuffed Chicken Breast

Prep Time: 10 minutes

Cooking time: 20 minutes

Servings: 7

Ingredients:

- ⅓ cup basil
- 3 ounces dry tomatoes
- 1-pound chicken breast
- 1 tablespoon olive oil
- 3 ounces dill
- 1 teaspoon paprika

- ½ teaspoon ground ginger
- 1 teaspoon salt
- ½ teaspoon ground coriander
- ½ teaspoon cayenne pepper
- 2 tablespoons lemon juice
- ¼ cup sour cream

Directions:

1. Wash the basil and chop it. Chop the dried tomatoes.

2. Mix the chopped ingredients in a suitable mixing bowl and sprinkle with the paprika and ground ginger and stir well.

3. Pound the prepared chicken breast with a mallet to flatten them.

4. Rub the chicken breast with the dill, salt, ground coriander, cayenne pepper, and lemon juice. Fill the chicken breast with the chopped basil mixture.

5. Set the Ninja Foodi to" Steam" mode. Spray the Ninja Foodi with olive oil. Spread the stuffed chicken breast with sour cream.

6. Close the chicken breasts with toothpicks and place them in the Ninja Foodi.

7. Close the Ninja Foodi's lid and cook for 20 minutes.

8. Once it is done, open the Ninja Foodi's lid and remove the chicken breast.

9. Remove the toothpicks, slice the stuffed chicken breast, and serve.

Nutrition Values Per Serving:

Calories: 179, Total fat: 9.4g, Fiber: 2g, Carbohydrates: 8.89g, Protein: 16g

Thai Chicken

Prep Time: 10 minutes

Cooking time: 35 minutes

Servings: 8

Ingredients:

- 14 ounces boneless chicken breast
- 1 teaspoon black pepper
- 1 teaspoon paprika
- 1 teaspoon turmeric
- 3 tablespoons fish sauce
- ½ teaspoon curry
- 1 teaspoon salt
- 3 tablespoons butter
- ¼ cup fresh basil
- 1 teaspoon olive oil

Directions:

1. Cut the boneless chicken breast into medium pieces.

2. Mix the black pepper, paprika, turmeric, curry, and salt in a suitable mixing bowl and stir well.

3. Toss the cut-up chicken pieces with the spice mixture and coat well.

4. Chop the basil and mix it with the butter in a small bowl.

5. Stir the mixture until smooth. Set the Ninja Foodi to" Sauté" mode.

6. Add the butter mixture into the Ninja Foodi. Melt it.

7. Transfer the chicken filets into the Ninja Foodi and sauté them for 10 minutes.

8. Add the olive oil and fish sauce.

9. Close the Ninja Foodi's lid and cook the dish on "Sear/Sauté" mode for 25 minutes.

10. Once cooked, remove the chicken from the Ninja Foodi.

11. Let the dish rest briefly and serve.

Nutrition Values Per Serving:

Calories: 182, Total fat: 12g, Fiber: 1g, Carbohydrates: 12.7g, Protein: 6g

Creamy Chicken Pancake

Prep Time: 20 minutes

Cooking time: 15 minutes

Servings: 9

Ingredients:

- 1 cup flour
- 3 eggs
- 1 teaspoon salt
- 1 teaspoon psyllium husk powder
- ½ cup half and half
- ½ tablespoon baking soda
- 1 tablespoon apple cider vinegar
- 1 medium onion
- ½ teaspoon black pepper
- 7 ounces ground chicken
- 1 teaspoon paprika
- 1 tablespoon tomato paste
- 1 tablespoon butter
- 1 tablespoon olive oil
- 1 tablespoon sour cream

Directions:

1. Beat the eggs in a suitable mixing bowl, add half and half and flour, and whisk until smooth batter forms.

2. Add the baking soda, salt, apple cider vinegar, and psyllium husk powder, and stir well.

3. Let the prepared batter rest for 10 minutes in the refrigerator.

4. Peel the onion and dice it. Mix the ground chicken with the black pepper, paprika, tomato paste, kosher salt, and sour cream in a suitable mixing bowl and stir well.

5. Set the Ninja Foodi to" Sauté" mode. Add the ground chicken mixture and sauté the meat for 10 minutes, stirring frequently.

6. Remove the chicken from the Ninja Foodi. Pour the sesame oil and begin to cook the pancakes.

7. Ladle a small amount of the batter into the Ninja Foodi.

8. Cook the chicken pancakes for 1 minute per side.

9. Place one pancake into the Ninja Foodi and spread it with the ground chicken.

10. Repeat the step until you form a pancake cake.

11. Close the Ninja's lid and cook the dish on" Pressure" mode for 10 minutes.

12. Once cooked, remove the cake from the Ninja Foodi and let it rest briefly.

13. Cut into slices and serve.

Nutrition Values Per Serving:

Calories: 134, Total fat: 9.4g, Fiber: 1g, Carbohydrates: 3.4g, Protein: 9.6g

Sriracha Chicken Satay

Prep Time: 10 minutes

Cooking time: 16 minutes

Servings: 8

Ingredients:

- 10 ounces boneless chicken thighs
- ½ cup sweet soy sauce
- ½ cup dark soy sauce
- 1 teaspoon lemongrass paste
- 1 tablespoon almond oil
- 1 teaspoon salt
- 1 tablespoon scallions
- ½ tablespoon sriracha

Directions:

1. Chop the chicken thighs and sprinkle them with the lemongrass paste and salt and stir well.

2. Set the Ninja Foodi to" Pressure" mode. Place the chicken thighs into the Ninja Foodi and add the soy sauces.

3. Chop the scallions and add them into the Ninja Foodi.

4. Top the mixture with the sriracha and almond oil, stir well using a spoon and Close the Ninja's lid.

5. Cook on "Pressure" mode for 16 minutes at high.

6. Once cooked, release the pressure and open the lid.

7. Transfer the cooked chicken satay to a serving plate and sprinkle it with the sauce from the Ninja Foodi.

8. Serve the dish hot.

Nutrition Values Per Serving:

Calories: 85, Total fat: 4.7g, Fiber: 0g, Carbohydrates: 1.98g, Protein: 9g

Saucy Chicken Breast

Prep Time: 15 minutes

Cooking time: 40 minutes

Servings: 8

Ingredients:

- 2 pounds of chicken breasts
- 2 tablespoons ketchup
- ½ cup Sugar

- ⅓ cup of soy sauce
- 1 teaspoon salt
- 2 ounces fresh rosemary
- 1 teaspoon ground white pepper
- ¼ cup garlic
- 2 tablespoons olive oil
- 1 white onion
- 4 tablespoons water
- 1 tablespoon flax meal
- ⅓ teaspoon red Chilli flakes
- 1 teaspoon oregano

Directions:

1. Place the chicken breast into the Ninja Foodi. Set the Ninja Foodi to" Pressure" mode.

2. Mix the ketchup, sugar, soy sauce, salt, rosemary, and ground white pepper in a suitable mixing bowl and whisk until smooth.

3. Peel the garlic and white onion, and then slice the vegetables.

4. Mix the sliced vegetables with the chile flakes and oregano and stir.

5. Place Sugar mixture into the Ninja Foodi. Mix well, Close the Ninja's lid, and cook for 10 minutes.

6. Mix flax meal with water in a suitable mixing bowl.

7. Once it is done, release the cooker's pressure and open the lid.

8. Remove the chicken breast from the Ninja Foodi and chop it.

9. Pour the starch mixture into the Ninja Foodi and stir. Add the chicken and Close the Ninja's lid.

10. Cook the chicken on "Sauté" mode for 30 minutes.

11. Once it is done, remove the dish from the Ninja Foodi, let it rest briefly, and serve.

Nutrition Values Per Serving:

Calories: 295, Total fat: 13.4g, Fiber: 3.9g, Carbohydrates: 9.5g, Protein: 34.6g

Chicken Cheese Bowl

Prep Time: 15 minutes

Cooking time: 30 minutes

Servings: 6

Ingredients:

- 7 ounces Feta cheese
- 10 ounces boneless chicken breast
- 1 teaspoon basil
- 1 tablespoon onion powder
- 1 teaspoon olive oil
- 1 tablespoon sesame oil
- 4 ounces green olives
- 2 cucumbers
- 1 cup of water

- 1 teaspoon salt

Directions:

1. Set the Ninja Foodi to" Pressure" mode.
2. Place the boneless chicken breast into the Ninja Foodi.
3. Add water, basil, and onion powder, stir well and Close the Ninja's lid.
4. Cook on "Pressure" mode at High for 30 minutes.
5. Chop the Feta cheese roughly and sprinkle it with olive oil.
6. Slice the green olives. Chop the cucumbers into medium-sized cubes.
7. Mix the chopped cheese, sliced green olives, and cucumbers in a suitable mixing bowl.
8. Top the mixture with salt and sesame oil.
9. When the chicken is cooked, open the Ninja Foodi and remove it from the machine.
10. Allow the chicken to cool a little and chop roughly.
11. Return this chicken to the cheese mixture.
12. Mix well and serve.

Nutrition Values Per Serving:

Calories: 279, Total fat: 19.8g, Fiber: 2g, Carbohydrates: 15.37g, Protein: 11g

Duck Meat Tacos

Prep Time: 10 minutes

Cooking time: 22 minutes

Servings: 7

Ingredients:

- 1-pound duck breast fillet
- 1 teaspoon salt
- 1 teaspoon Chilli powder
- 1 teaspoon onion powder
- 1 teaspoon oregano
- 1 teaspoon basil
- 1 cup lettuce
- 1 teaspoon black pepper
- 1 tablespoon tomato sauce
- 1 cup chicken stock
- 1 tablespoon olive oil
- 6 ounces Cheddar cheese
- 7 flour tortilla
- 1 teaspoon turmeric

Directions:

1. Chop the duck fillet and transfer it to the blender.
2. Blend the mixture well. Set the Ninja Foodi to" Sauté" mode.
3. Place the blended duck fillet into the Ninja Foodi.
4. Sprinkle it with olive oil and stir well. Sauté the dish for 5 minutes.

5. Mix the salt, Chilli powder, onion powder, oregano, basil, black pepper, and turmeric in a suitable mixing bowl and stir.

6. Add tomato sauce. Sprinkle the blended duck fillet with the spice mixture.

7. Mix well and add chicken stock. Stir gently and Close the Ninja's lid.

8. Cook the mixture at the" Pressure" mode for 17 minutes.

9. Wash the lettuce and chop it roughly. Grate the Cheddar cheese.

10. When the duck mixture is cooked, remove it from the Ninja Foodi and let it rest briefly.

11. Place the chopped lettuce in the tortillas.

12. Add the duck mixture to tortillas and top it with grated cheese.

13. Serve.

Nutrition Values Per Serving:

Calories: 246, Total fat: 12.9g, Fiber: 1.6g, Carbohydrates: 4.1g, Protein: 28.9g

Salsa Verde Dipped Chicken

Prep Time: 10 minutes

Cooking time: 30 minutes

Servings: 6

Ingredients:

- 10 ounces Salsa Verde
- 1 tablespoon paprika
- 1-pound boneless chicken breasts
- 1 teaspoon salt
- 1 teaspoon ground coriander
- 1 teaspoon cilantro

Directions:

1. Rub the boneless chicken breasts with paprika, salt, black pepper, and cilantro. Set the Ninja Foodi to" Pressure" mode.

2. Place the boneless chicken into the Ninja Foodi.

3. Sprinkle the meat with the salsa Verde and stir well.

4. Close the Ninja Foodi's lid and cook for 30 minutes.

5. Once it is done, release the pressure and transfer the chicken to the mixing bowl.

6. Shred the chicken well and serve.

Nutrition Values Per Serving:

Calories: 222, Total fat: 11.3g, Fiber: 3g, Carbohydrates: 21.02g, Protein: 9g

Onions Stuffed with Chicken

Prep Time: 15 minutes

Cooking time: 40 minutes

Servings: 5

Ingredients:

- 5 large white onions, chopped

- 1-pound ground chicken
- 1 cup cream
- 1 cup chicken stock
- 1 teaspoon salt
- 1 teaspoon oregano
- 1 teaspoon basil
- 1 egg
- 1 teaspoon turmeric
- 5 garlic cloves

Directions:

1. Place the ground chicken in a suitable mixing bowl and sprinkle it with salt, oregano, basil, and turmeric.

2. Stir in egg and mix well evenly.

3. Set the Ninja Foodi to" Sear/Sauté" mode. Transfer the stuffed onions to the Ninja Foodi.

4. Add the chicken stock and cream. Close the Ninja's lid and cook for 40 minutes.

5. Once it is done, open the lid and let the onions sit for 2 minutes.

6. Transfer the stuffed onions to a serving plate and sprinkle them with the liquid from the Ninja Foodi.

7. Serve warm.

Nutrition Values Per Serving:

Calories: 318, Total fat: 19.3g, Fiber: 2g, Carbohydrates: 15.56g, Protein: 22g

Chicken Cutlets

Prep Time: 10 minutes

Cooking time: 25 minutes

Servings: 8

Ingredients:

- 14 ounces ground chicken
- 1 teaspoon black pepper
- 1 teaspoon paprika
- 1 teaspoon cilantro
- 1 teaspoon oregano
- ½ teaspoon minced garlic
- 2 tablespoons starch
- 1 teaspoon red chile flakes
- 1 tablespoon oatmeal flour
- 1 egg

Directions:

1. Place the ground chicken in a suitable mixing bowl.

2. Sprinkle it with black pepper, cilantro, and oregano.

3. Add paprika and minced garlic and mix using your hands.

4. Beat the egg in a separate bowl.

5. Add the starch and oatmeal flour to the egg and stir well until smooth.

6. Add the egg mixture to the ground meat.

7. Add the Chilli flakes and mix well. Make the medium cutlets from the ground chicken mixture.

8. Set the Ninja Foodi to" Steam" mode.

9. Transfer the chicken cutlets to the Ninja Foodi trivet and place the trivet into the Ninja Foodi.

10. Close the Ninja's lid and cook the chicken cutlets on Steam mode for 25 minutes.

11. Once cooked, remove the food from the Ninja Foodi, let it rest, and serve.

Nutrition Values Per Serving:

Calories: 96, Total fat: 5.3g, Fiber: 0g, Carbohydrates: 1.89g, Protein: 10g

Savory Pulled Chicken

Prep Time: 10 minutes

Cooking time: 22 minutes

Servings: 7

Ingredients

- 1-pound chicken breast, boneless
- 1 tablespoon Sugar
- 1 teaspoon black pepper
- 1 teaspoon olive oil
- 2 cups of water
- 1 ounce's bay leaf
- 1 tablespoon basil
- 1 tablespoon butter
- ½ cup cream
- 1 teaspoon salt
- 3 garlic cloves
- 1 teaspoon turmeric

Directions:

1. Set the Ninja Foodi to" Pressure" mode.

2. Pour water into the Ninja Foodi and add the chicken breast.

3. Add the bay leaf. Close the Ninja's lid and cook for 12 minutes.

4. Once it is done, release the cooker's pressure and open the Ninja Foodi's lid.

5. Transfer the chicken breast to a mixing bowl and shred it.

6. Sprinkle the shredded chicken with sugar, black pepper, basil, butter, cream, salt, and turmeric and stir well.

7. Peel the garlic cloves and mince them.

8. Spray the Ninja Foodi with the olive oil inside and transfer the shredded chicken into a Ninja Foodi.

9. Cook the dish on" Sauté" mode for 10 minutes.

10. Once cooked, transfer it to a serving plate.

11. Devour

Nutrition Values Per Serving:

Calories: 122, Total fat: 5.3g, Fiber: 1.3g, Carbohydrates: 4.4g, Protein: 14.4g

Chicken with Pomegranate Sauce

Prep Time: 10 minutes

Cooking time: 29 minutes

Servings: 6

Ingredients:

- ½ cup pomegranate juice
- 2 tablespoons Sugar
- 1 teaspoon cinnamon
- ¼ cup chicken stock
- 2 pounds of chicken breast
- 1 teaspoon starch
- 1 teaspoon butter
- 1 tablespoon oregano
- 1 teaspoon turmeric
- ½ teaspoon red chili flakes

Directions:

1. Set the Ninja Foodi to" Pressure" mode. Put the chicken breast into the Ninja Foodi and sprinkle it with oregano, butter, chicken stock, and chile flakes.

2. Stir the mixture and close the Ninja Foodi's lid. Cook the meat for 20 minutes.

3. Mix the pomegranate juice, sugar, cinnamon, starch, and turmeric and stir well until everything is dissolved.

4. Once it is done, open the Ninja Foodi's lid and remove the chicken.

5. Set the Ninja Foodi to" Sauté" mode.

6. Pour the pomegranate sauce into the Ninja Foodi and sauté it for 4 minutes.

7. Return the chicken back into the Ninja Foodi and stir the dish using a spoon.

8. Close the Ninja's lid and cook the chicken in" Pressure" mode for 5 minutes.

9. Once it is done, release the cooker's pressure then remove the Ninja Foodi's lid.

10. Transfer the juicy chicken to a serving plate.

11. Drizzle the pomegranate sauce on top.

Nutrition Values Per Serving:

Calories: 198, Total fat: 4.6g, Fiber: 0.6g, Carbohydrates: 4.7g, Protein: 32.2g

Baked Parmesan Chicken

Prep Time: 10 minutes

Cooking time: 30 minutes

Servings: 8

Ingredients:

- 1 cup tomato, chopped
- 3 tablespoons butter

- 1-pound boneless chicken breast
- 1 teaspoon salt
- 1 teaspoon paprika
- 7 ounces Parmesan cheese
- ½ cup fresh basil
- 1 teaspoon cilantro
- 1 tablespoon sour cream

Directions:

1. Grate the Parmesan cheese, mix it with the cilantro and paprika in a suitable mixing bowl, and stir.
2. Sprinkle the boneless chicken breast with the salt and place it into the Ninja Foodi.
3. Add the basil, butter, tomato, and sour cream.
4. Sprinkle the chicken with the grated cheese mixture and Close the Ninja's lid.
5. Cook the chicken on "Pressure" mode for 30 minutes at High.
6. Once it is done, release the cooker's pressure then remove the Ninja Foodi's lid.
7. Transfer the dish to a serving plate.

Nutrition Values Per Serving:

Calories: 234, Total fat: 14.2g, Fiber: 0.4g, Carbohydrates: 2g, Protein: 24.8g

Seasoned Chicken Strips

Prep Time: 10 minutes

Cooking time: 8 minutes

Servings: 7

Ingredients:

- 1 cup flour
- 1 teaspoon kosher salt
- 1 teaspoon cayenne pepper
- ½ teaspoon cilantro
- ½ teaspoon oregano
- ½ teaspoon paprika
- ½ cup of coconut milk
- 1-pound chicken fillet
- 3 tablespoons sesame oil
- 1 teaspoon turmeric

Directions:

1. Place the flour in a suitable mixing bowl.
2. Add kosher salt, cayenne pepper, cilantro, oregano, paprika, and turmeric and mix well.
3. Pour the coconut milk into a separate bowl. Cut the chicken into strips.
4. Set the Ninja Foodi to" Sauté" mode. Pour the olive oil into the Ninja Foodi.
5. Dip the chicken strips in the coconut milk, then dip them in the flour mixture.
6. Repeat this step two more times.

7. Add the dipped chicken strips to the Ninja Foodi.

8. Sauté the chicken strips for 3 minutes on each side.

9. Transfer the chicken to a paper towel to drain any excess oil before serving.

10. Serve warm.

Nutrition Values Per Serving:

Calories: 244, Total fat: 18.1g, Fiber: 1.6g, Carbohydrates: 10.6g, Protein: 11.9g

Herbed Chicken Wings

Prep Time: 10 minutes

Cooking time: 20 minutes

Servings: 7

Ingredients:

- 4 tablespoons dry dill
- 1 cup Greek yogurt
- 1 teaspoon salt
- 1 teaspoon black pepper
- ½ teaspoon red chile flakes
- 1 teaspoon oregano
- 1 tablespoon olive oil
- 1-pound chicken wings
- 1 teaspoon lemon juice

Directions:

1. Mix the yogurt, salt, black pepper, Chilli flakes, oregano, and lemon juice in a suitable mixing bowl, blending until smooth.

2. Add 2 tbsp dill and stir well. Add the chicken wings and coat them with the yogurt mixture.

3. Let the chicken wings rest for 2 hours.

4. Set the Ninja Foodi to "Pressure" mode. Pour the olive oil into the Ninja Foodi.

5. Add the chicken wings. Sprinkle the chicken wings with the remaining dill.

6. Close the Ninja Foodi and cook for 20 minutes.

7. Once the wings are cooked, then remove them from the Ninja Foodi.

8. Let the wings rest briefly and serve.

Nutrition Values Per Serving:

Calories: 122, Total fat: 4.5g, Fiber: 1g, Carbohydrates: 2.77g, Protein: 17g

Cheesy Chicken Fillets

Prep Time: 10 minutes

Cooking time: 15 minutes

Servings: 7

Ingredients:

- 1 cup cream cheese
- 6 ounces Cheddar cheese

- 1 yellow onion
- 14 ounces boneless chicken breast
- 1 teaspoon olive oil
- 1 tablespoon black pepper
- 1 teaspoon red chile flakes
- 4 ounces apricot, pitted
- 3 tablespoons chicken stock

Directions:

1. Cut the chicken breast into fillets and sprinkle the boneless chicken breasts with the black pepper, olive oil, and chile flakes.

2. Set the Ninja Foodi to" Sauté" mode. Transfer the chicken breasts into the Ninja Foodi and sauté for 5 minutes per side.

3. Meanwhile, grate the Cheddar cheese and mix it with the cream cheese.

4. Add chicken stock and mix well using a spoon.

5. Mix apricots with sliced onions in a bowl.

6. Once it is done, open the Ninja Foodi's lid.

7. Sprinkle the chicken with the onion mixture.

8. Add the Cheddar cheese mixture.

9. close the Ninja's lid and cook at the" Pressure" mode for 10 minutes.

10. Once it is done, release the cooker's pressure and open the Ninja Foodi's lid.

11. Transfer the chicken to the serving plates.

Nutrition Values Per Serving:

Calories: 282, Total fat: 18.1g, Fiber: 1g, Carbohydrates: 11.88g, Protein: 18g

BBQ Chicken Meatballs

Prep Time: 10 minutes

Cooking time: 25 minutes

Servings: 8

Ingredients:

- ⅓ cup BBQ sauce
- 1 teaspoon salt
- 1 teaspoon sugar
- 3 tablespoons chives
- 12 ounces ground chicken
- 1 egg
- 1 tablespoon coconut flour
- 1 tablespoon olive oil
- 1 teaspoon oregano
- 1 red onion

Directions:

1. Put the ground chicken in a suitable mixing bowl.

2. Sprinkle the ground meat with sugar, salt, chives, coconut flour, and oregano.

3. Peel the red onion, dice it, and add the onion to the ground chicken mixture.

4. Beat the egg in a suitable bowl and add it to the ground chicken.

5. Mix everything well using your hands until smooth.

6. Make small balls from the ground chicken.

7. Set the Ninja Foodi to" Sauté" mode. Pour the olive oil into the Ninja Foodi.

8. Put the chicken balls in the Ninja Foodi and sauté them for 5 minutes.

9. Stir them constantly to make all the sides of the chicken balls are brown.

10. Pour the barbecue sauce into the Ninja Foodi and Close the Ninja's lid.

11. Cook the dish on "Sear/Sauté" mode for 20 minutes.

12. Once it is done, remove the dish from the Ninja Foodi and serve.

Nutrition Values Per Serving:

Calories: 131, Total fat: 5.7g, Fiber: 0.8g, Carbohydrates: 6.3g, Protein: 13.3g

Chicken Dumplings

Prep Time: 10 minutes

Cooking time: 25 minutes

Servings: 7

Ingredients:

- 1 teaspoon salt
- ¼ teaspoon Sugar
- 1 cup flour
- ¼ cup whey
- 10 oz boneless chicken breast
- 1 tablespoon olive oil
- 1 cup of water
- 1 onion
- 1 teaspoon black pepper
- 1 teaspoon paprika

Directions:

1. Mix salt, sugar, and flour in a suitable mixing bowl and stir.

2. Add the whey and mix well. Knead the dough.

3. Make a long log from the dough and cut it into small dumpling pieces.

4. Chop the chicken roughly and sprinkle it with the black pepper.

5. Place the chopped chicken into the Ninja Foodi.

6. Set the Ninja Foodi to" Pressure" mode.

7. Sprinkle the chopped chicken with olive oil and add water.

8. Close the Ninja Foodi's lid and cook for 15 minutes. Peel the onion and slice it.

9. Once it is done, release the cooker's pressure and open the Ninja Foodi's lid.

10. Remove the cooked chicken and shred it. Return the chicken back to the Ninja Foodi.

11. Add the dumplings and sliced onion. Sprinkle the dish with paprika.

12. Close the Ninja Foodi's lid and cook the dish on" Pressure" mode for 10 minutes.

13. Once it is done, remove the dish from the Ninja Foodi, let it rest briefly, and serve.

Nutrition Values Per Serving:

Calories: 133, Total fat: 7.1g, Fiber: 1g, Carbohydrates: 4.5g, Protein: 13.1g

Chicken Rissoles

Prep Time: 10 minutes

Cooking time: 15 minutes

Servings: 8

Ingredients:

- 4 egg yolks
- 1 tablespoon turmeric
- 1 teaspoon salt
- 1 teaspoon dried parsley
- 1 tablespoon cream
- 12 ounces ground chicken
- 1 tablespoon almond oil
- 1 tablespoon sesame seeds
- 1 teaspoon minced garlic

Directions:

1. Mix the turmeric, salt, dried parsley, and sesame seeds in a suitable mixing bowl.
2. Beat egg yolks in a mini bowl and pour in to the ground chicken in a large bowl.
3. Add the spice mixture and garlic and combine.
4. Make small rissoles from the ground chicken mixture. Set the Ninja Foodi to" Sauté" mode.
5. Pour the olive oil into the Ninja Foodi and add the chicken rissoles.
6. Sauté the chicken rissoles for 15 minutes, stirring frequently.
7. Once cooked, serve.

Nutrition Values Per Serving:

Calories: 117, Total fat: 8.4g, Fiber: 0g, Carbohydrates: 1.42g, Protein: 9g

Chicken Broth with Fresh Herbs

Prep Time: 10 minutes

Cooking time: 45 minutes

Servings: 13

Ingredients:

- 8 ounces drumsticks
- 8 ounces of chicken wings
- ⅓ cup fresh thyme
- ¼ cup fresh dill
- ¼ cup fresh parsley
- 1 teaspoon black pepper

- 10 cups water
- 1 teaspoon salt
- 2 tablespoons fresh rosemary
- 1 garlic clove
- 1 onion

Directions:

1. Wash the drumsticks and chicken wings carefully.
2. Chop them roughly and transfer the ingredients to the Ninja Foodi.
3. Set the Ninja Foodi to" Sauté" mode. Top the mixture with the salt and black pepper and stir well using your hands.
4. Wash the thyme, dill, and parsley and chop them. Put the chopped greens into the Ninja Foodi.
5. Add water and rosemary. Peel the onion and garlic.
6. Add the vegetables to the chicken mixture.
7. Close the Ninja Foodi's lid and cook the dish for 45 minutes.
8. Once it is done, discard the greens from the Ninja Foodi.
9. Remove the chicken from the Ninja Foodi.
10. Strain the chicken stock and serve it with the cooked chicken.
11. Serve warm.

Nutrition Values Per Serving:

Calories: 35, Total fat: 0.7g, Fiber: 1g, Carbohydrates: 3.06g, Protein: 4g

Peanut Butter Duck

Prep Time: 10 minutes

Cooking time: 25 minutes

Servings: 6

Ingredients:

- 4 tablespoons creamy peanut butter
- ½ cup fresh dill
- 1 teaspoon oregano
- 1 tablespoon lemon juice
- 1 teaspoon lime zest
- ¼ teaspoon cinnamon
- 1 teaspoon turmeric
- 1 teaspoon paprika
- ½ teaspoon cumin
- ½ teaspoon black pepper
- 1 cup chicken stock
- 1 tablespoon butter
- 1-pound duck breast
- ¼ cup red wine

Directions:

1. Mix the chopped dill with the lime zest, cinnamon, turmeric, lemon juice, paprika, cumin, and black pepper and stir well.

2. Set the Ninja Foodi to" Pressure" mode.

3. Rub the duck with the spice mixture and place it into the Ninja Foodi.

4. Sprinkle the meat with oregano. Add the chicken stock, red wine, and butter.

5. Close the Ninja Foodi's lid and cook on "Pressure" mode for 18 minutes at High.

6. Once it is done, release the cooker's pressure then remove the Ninja Foodi's lid.

7. Set the Ninja Foodi to" Sauté" mode. Remove the dish from the Ninja Foodi.

8. Add the peanut butter into the Ninja Foodi and sauté it for 1 minute.

9. Add the duck and sauté the dish for 5 minutes.

10. Stir the duck a couple of times.

11. Once done, transfer the duck to a serving plate and let it rest briefly before serving.

Nutrition Values Per Serving:

Calories: 198, Total fat: 11.5g, Fiber: 1g, Carbohydrates: 4.74g, Protein: 19g

Creamy Chicken Dip

Prep Time: 15 minutes

Cooking time: 30 minutes

Servings: 8

Ingredients:

- 2 tablespoons miso paste
- 1 teaspoon liquid stevia
- 1 teaspoon apple cider vinegar
- ¼ cup cream
- ½ teaspoon white pepper
- 3 tablespoons chicken stock
- 7 ounces boneless chicken breast
- 1 teaspoon black-eyed peas
- 3 cups of water

Directions:

1. Chop the chicken breast roughly and place it into the Ninja Foodi.

2. Set the Ninja Foodi to "Sear/Sauté" mode. Add water, black-eyed peas, and white pepper.

3. Stir the mixture and Close the Ninja's lid. Cook the dish on poultry mode for 30 minutes.

4. Mix the miso paste and chicken stock in a suitable mixing bowl.

5. Add liquid stevia and apple cider vinegar.

6. Whisk the mixture carefully until miso paste is dissolved.

7. When the chicken is cooked, remove it from the Ninja Foodi and let it rest briefly.

8. Transfer the chicken to a blender and add cream.

9. Blend the mixture for 5 minutes or until smooth.

10. Add the miso paste mixture and blend the mixture for 1 minute.

11. Transfer the cooked chicken dip to a serving dish and serve.

Nutrition Values Per Serving:

Calories: 62, Total fat: 2.5g, Fiber: 0.3g, Carbohydrates: 1.6g, Protein: 7.8g

Crispy Duck Cutlets

Prep Time: 10 minutes

Cooking time: 20 minutes

Servings: 8

Ingredients:

- ¼ cup vermouth
- 1-pound ground duck
- 1 teaspoon salt
- 4 ounces keto bread
- ¼ cup cream
- 1 teaspoon paprika
- 1 teaspoon coconut flour
- 1 teaspoon white pepper

Directions:

1. Mix the ground duck and vermouth in a suitable mixing bowl.
2. Chop the bread and mix it with the cream and stir well until smooth.
3. Use a blender, if necessary. Add the bread mixture to the ground duck.
4. Sprinkle the meat mixture with salt, paprika, and white pepper.
5. Add coconut flour and mix well using a spoon.
6. Make the medium cutlets from the duck mixture and transfer them to the trivet.
7. Set the Ninja Foodi to" Steam" mode.
8. Place the Ninja's trivet into the Ninja Foodi and Close the Ninja's lid.
9. Cook the dish on steam mode for 20 minutes.
10. Once it is done, remove the cutlets from the Ninja Foodi. Rest briefly and serve.

Nutrition Values Per Serving:

Calories: 121, Total fat: 5.4g, Fiber: 1.4g, Carbohydrates: 4.9g, Protein: 12.3g

Creamy Chicken Soup

Prep Time: 15 minutes

Cooking time: 22 minutes

Servings: 8

Ingredients:

- 4 cups of water
- 2 cups cream
- ⅓ cup half and half
- 1 tablespoon minced garlic
- 5 ounces mushrooms, chopped
- 1 onion

- 1 tablespoon olive oil
- ½ tablespoon salt
- 1 teaspoon fresh basil
- 1 teaspoon fresh dill
- 7 ounces chicken breast

Directions:

1. Peel the onion. Set the Ninja Foodi to" Sauté" mode.
2. Transfer the onion and mushroom to the Ninja Foodi and add olive oil.
3. Sauté the vegetable mixture for 5 minutes, stirring constantly.
4. Add chicken and cream. Add the half and half and water.
5. Top the mixture with garlic, salt, dill, and basil, stir well, and Close the Ninja's lid.
6. Cook the dish for 20 minutes in the" Pressure" mode.
7. Open the Ninja Foodi's lid and remove the chicken breast and shred it.
8. Blend the soup mixture using an immersion blender until smooth.
9. Add the shredded chicken and close the Ninja Foodi's lid.
10. Cook the soup at the" Pressure" mode for 2 minutes.
11. Ladle the cooked soup into serving bowls.

Nutrition Values Per Serving:

Calories: 106, Total fat: 6.9g, Fiber: 0.5g, Carbohydrates: 4.6g, Protein: 6.9g

Spicy Pulled Duck

Prep Time: 10 minutes

Cooking time: 27 minutes

Servings: 8

Ingredients:

- ⅓ cup red wine
- 1/2 cup chicken stock
- 1 teaspoon onion powder
- 14 ounces duck fillet
- 2 teaspoons cayenne pepper
- ¼ teaspoon minced garlic
- ⅓ cup fresh dill
- 1 teaspoon salt
- 1 teaspoon black pepper
- 1 tablespoon sour cream
- 1 tablespoon tomato puree

Directions:

1. Mix the red wine and chicken stock in a suitable mixing bowl and stir.
2. Set the Ninja Foodi to" Sauté" mode.
3. Pour the chicken stock mixture into the Ninja Foodi and preheat it for 1 minute.
4. Mix the onion powder, cayenne pepper, salt, black pepper, and garlic in a suitable mixing bowl.

5. Stir the mixture and sprinkle the duck fillet with the spice mixture.

6. Place the duck fillet into the Ninja Foodi and Close the Ninja's lid.

7. Cook the duck on" Pressure" mode for 25 minutes at High.

8. Once it is done, remove the dish from the Ninja Foodi and let it rest briefly.

9. Shred the duck using a fork. Leave a third of the liquid into the Ninja Foodi and return the shredded duck.

10. Add the tomato puree and sour cream. Chop the dill and sprinkle the dish with it.

11. Stir it gently and Close the Ninja's lid.

12. Cook the dish on" Sauté" mode for 2 minutes.

13. Once it is done, transfer the hot dish to a serving plate and serve.

Nutrition Values Per Serving:

Calories: 119, Total fat: 7.9g, Fiber: 0g, Carbohydrates: 1.81g, Protein: 9g

Oregano Chicken Drumsticks

Prep Time: 5 minutes

Cooking time: 18 minutes

Servings: 7

Ingredients:

- 1-pound chicken drumsticks
- 1 teaspoon salt
- 1 teaspoon paprika
- 1 teaspoon white pepper
- 1 cup of water
- 1 teaspoon thyme
- ½ teaspoon oregano

Directions:

1. Sprinkle the chicken drumsticks with salt, paprika, thyme, oregano, and white pepper and stir well.

2. Set the Ninja Foodi to" Pressure" mode at High.

3. Place the chicken drumsticks into the Ninja Foodi and add the water.

4. Close the Ninja's lid and cook for 18 minutes.

5. Once it is done, release the cooker's pressure and open the Ninja Foodi's lid.

6. Remove the drumsticks from the Ninja Foodi and transfer them to the serving platter.

Nutrition Values Per Serving:

Calories: 112, Total fat: 3.8g, Fiber: 0g, Carbohydrates: 0.5g, Protein: 17.9g

Creamy Chicken Stew

Prep Time: 15 minutes

Cooking time: 35 minutes

Servings: 8

Ingredients

- ½ cup tomato juice
- 1 tablespoon sugar
- 1 teaspoon salt
- 1-pound boneless chicken breast
- 1 tablespoon oregano
- 1 teaspoon cilantro
- 1 teaspoon fresh ginger, peeled and chopped
- 2 carrots, peeled and chopped
- 3 red onion, peeled and chopped
- 5 ounces shallot, chopped
- 1 tablespoon black pepper
- ½ cup cream
- 3 cups chicken stock
- 3 ounces scallions, chopped
- 2 tablespoons olive oil
- 3 ounces eggplants, peeled and chopped

Directions:

1. Mix the tomato juice with the oregano, salt, black pepper, cilantro, and cream in a suitable mixing bowl and stir.
2. Set the Ninja Foodi to" Sauté" mode.
3. Add chopped vegetables to the Ninja Foodi and drizzle olive oil.
4. Sauté these vegetables for 5 minutes.
5. Add the tomato juice mixture and the rest of the ingredients to the pot.
6. Stir well using a spoon and close the Ninja Foodi's lid.
7. Cook chicken on" Pressure" mode for 30 minutes.
8. Release the pressure naturally, then remove the lid.
9. Serve warm.

Nutrition Values Per Serving:

Calories: 205, Total fat: 9g, Fiber: 2.5g, Carbohydrates: 13.7g, Protein: 18.4g

Baked Chicken Bread

Prep Time: 15 minutes

Cooking time: 40 minutes

Servings: 8

Ingredients:

- ½ tablespoon garam masala powder
- 8 ounces keto dough
- 1 teaspoon sesame seeds
- 1 egg yolk
- 1 teaspoon ground cilantro
- 1 teaspoon dill

- 10 ounces ground chicken
- ¼ cup fresh parsley
- 1 teaspoon olive oil
- 1 tablespoon black pepper
- 1 onion

Directions:

1. Roll the dough using a rolling pin. Mix the ground chicken with the ground cilantro and black pepper and stir well.

2. Wash the parsley carefully and chop it. Add the parsley to the chicken mixture.

3. Peel the onion and dice it. Add the onion to the chicken mixture.

4. Mix the meat mixture using your hands. Set the Ninja Foodi to" Pressure" mode.

5. Place the ground meat mixture in the middle of the rolled dough.

6. Wrap the dough in the shape of the bread.

7. Spray the Ninja Foodi with the olive oil inside and put the chicken bread there.

8. Whisk the egg yolk and sprinkle the chicken bread with it.

9. Sprinkle the dish with sesame seeds.

10. Close the Ninja Foodi's lid and cook the dish for 40 minutes.

11. Once it is done, open the Ninja Foodi's lid and check to see if the dish is cooked using a toothpick.

12. Transfer the chicken bread to a serving plate and let it rest briefly.

13. Slice it and serve.

Nutrition Values Per Serving:

Calories: 189, Total fat: 5.3g, Fiber: 4.2g, Carbohydrates: 8.1g, Protein: 27.3g

Zesty Duck Legs

Prep Time: 10 minutes

Cooking time: 25minutes

Servings: 6

Ingredients:

- 1-pound duck legs
- ½ cup pomegranate juice
- ½ cup dill
- 1 teaspoon salt
- 1 teaspoon black pepper
- 1 teaspoon ground ginger
- 1 tablespoon olive oil
- ½ cup of water
- 1 teaspoon brown sugar
- 1 tablespoon lime zest
- 2 teaspoons soy sauce
- ⅓ teaspoon peppercorn

Directions:

1. Mix the black pepper, salt, lime zest, ground ginger, brown sugar, and peppercorn in a suitable mixing bowl and stir well.

2. Sprinkle the duck legs with the spice mixture and mix well using your hands.

3. Add the soy sauce, water, olive oil, and pomegranate juice.

4. Wash the dill and chop it. Sprinkle the duck legs mixture with the chopped dill.

5. Set the Ninja Foodi to" Pressure" mode at High.

6. Transfer the duck legs mixture into the Ninja Foodi and Close the Ninja's lid.

7. Cook for 25 minutes. Once cooked, open the Ninja Foodi's lid and transfer the cooked duck legs to a serving dish.

8. Sprinkle the dish with the pomegranate sauce, if desired and serve

Nutrition Values Per Serving:

Calories: 209, Total fat: 11.4g, Fiber: 0g, Carbohydrates: 5.11g, Protein: 21g

Creamy Chicken Zoodles

Prep Time: 10 minutes

Cooking time: 27 minutes

Servings: 8

Ingredients:

- 5 ounces zoodles, cooked
- 1-pound boneless chicken breast
- 1 teaspoon cilantro
- 1 cup cream
- ⅓ cup chicken stock
- 1 teaspoon butter
- 1 teaspoon salt
- ½ cup cream cheese
- 1 teaspoon paprika
- 1 teaspoon garlic powder

Directions:

1. Mix the cilantro, salt, paprika, and garlic powder in a suitable mixing bowl and stir well.

2. Sprinkle the boneless chicken breast with the spice mixture and mix well using your hands.

3. Set the Ninja Foodi to" Pressure" mode. Place the spiced chicken into the Ninja Foodi.

4. Add cream, chicken stock, and cream cheese. Stir the mixture and close the Ninja Foodi's lid.

5. Cook the dish for 25 minutes. Open the lid and transfer the chicken to a mixing bowl.

6. Shred-it well using a fork. Transfer the shredded chicken into the Ninja Foodi.

7. Add cooked noodles, stir well, and Close the Ninja's lid.

8. Cook the zucchini noodles on" Pressure" mode for 2 minutes at High.

9. Remove the cooked dish from the Ninja Foodi. Serve it warm.

Nutrition Values Per Serving:

Calories: 186, Total fat: 18.9g, Fiber: 0.3g, Carbohydrates: 2.2g, Protein: 18g

Orange dipped Duck Breast

Prep Time: 10 minutes

Cooking time: 37minutes

Servings: 9

Ingredients:

- 2 pounds duck breast
- 2 oranges
- 2 tablespoons honey
- 1 cup of water
- 1 teaspoon cayenne pepper
- 1 teaspoon salt
- 1 teaspoon curry powder
- 2 tablespoons lemon juice
- 2 tablespoons butter
- 1 teaspoon sugar
- 1 teaspoon turmeric

Directions:

1. Make the zest from the oranges and chop the fruits.
2. Mix the orange zest and chopped oranges in a suitable mixing bowl.
3. Top the mixture with the honey, cayenne pepper, salt, curry powder, lemon juice, sugar, and turmeric and stir well.
4. Set the Ninja Foodi to" Sauté" mode. Put the duck in the orange mixture and stir it.
5. Add the butter into the Ninja Foodi and melt it at the sauté mode for 2 minutes.
6. Add water. Add the duck mixture and Close the Ninja's lid.
7. Set the Ninja Foodi mode to "Poultry" and cook the dish for 35 minutes.
8. Once it is done, open the Ninja Foodi's lid and remove the duck from the Ninja Foodi.
9. Slice and transfer the duck to a serving plate.
10. Sprinkle the cooked dish with the orange sauce from the Ninja Foodi and serve.

Nutrition Values Per Serving:

Calories: 174, Total fat: 7g, Fiber: 1g, Carbohydrates: 7.18g, Protein: 20g

Seafood Stew

Prep Time: 10 minutes

Cooking Time: 4 hours 50 minutes

Servings: 8

Ingredients:

- 2 tablespoons olive oil
- 1-pound tomatoes, chopped
- 1 large yellow onion, chopped finely
- 2 garlic cloves, minced
- 2 teaspoons curry powder
- 6 sprigs of fresh parsley
- Salt and black pepper, as required
- 1½ cups chicken broth
- 1½ pounds salmon, cut into cubes
- 1½ pounds shrimp, peeled and deveined

Directions:

1. Into the Ninja Foodi's pot of Ninja Foodi, add all ingredients except seafood and mix well.
2. Close the Ninja Foodi with a crisping lid and select "Slow Cook". Set on "High" for 4 hours.
3. Hit the "Start/Stop" button to initiate cooking.
4. Once done, pen the Ninja's lid and stir in the seafood.
5. Now, set on "Pressure" mode at Low for 50 minutes.
6. Hit the "Start/Stop" button to initiate cooking.
7. Open the lid and serve hot.

Nutrition Values Per Serving:

Calories: 272, Total fat: 10.7g, Fiber: 1.1g, Carbohydrates: 6g, Protein: 38g

Buttered Salmon Fillets

Prep Time: 10 minutes

Cooking Time: 10 minutes

Servings: 2

Ingredients:

- 2 (6-ounce) salmon fillets
- Salt and black pepper, as required
- 1 tablespoon butter, melted

Directions:

1. Arrange the greased Air Fryer Basket into the Ninja Foodi's pot of Ninja Foodi.
2. Season salmon fillet with butter, salt and black pepper.
3. Arrange the salmon fillets into the prepared Air Fryer Basket in a single layer.

4. Close the Ninja Foodi with a crisping lid and select "Air Crisp" mode.

5. Set the temperature to 360 degrees F temperature for almost 10 minutes.

6. Hit the "Start/Stop" button to initiate cooking.

7. Open the lid and serve hot.

Nutrition Values Per Serving:

Calories: 276, Total fat: 16.7g, Fiber: 0g, Carbohydrates: 12.06g, Protein: 33g

Creamy Salmon

Prep Time: 3 minutes

Cooking Time: 10 minutes

Servings: 2

Ingredients:

- 2 frozen salmon filets
- ½ cup of water
- 1 ½ teaspoons minced garlic
- ¼ cup heavy cream
- 1 cup parmesan cheese grated
- 1 tablespoon chopped fresh chives
- 1 tablespoon chopped fresh parsley
- 1 tablespoon fresh dill
- 1 teaspoon fresh lemon juice
- Salt and black pepper, to taste

Directions:

1. Add water and trivet to the pot. Place fillets on top of the trivet.

2. Close Ninja Foodi, press the pressure button, select high settings, and set the time to 4 minutes.

3. Once done cooking, do a quick release.

4. Transfer salmon to a serving plate. And remove trivet.

5. Press stop and then press the sauté button on Ninja Foodi.

6. Stir in heavy cream once the water begins to boil. Boil for 3 minutes.

7. Stir in lemon juice, parmesan cheese, dill, parsley, and chives.

8. Season with pepper and salt to taste

9. Serve and enjoy.

Nutrition Values Per Serving:

Calories: 423, Carbohydrates: 6.4g, Protein: 43.1g, Total fats 25.0g

Limed Haddock Fish

Prep Time: 15 minutes

Cooking Time: 25 minutes

Servings: 4

Ingredients:

- 1 garlic clove, minced

- ¼ teaspoon fresh ginger, grated finely
- ½ cup low-sodium soy sauce
- ¼ cup fresh lime juice
- ½ cup chicken broth
- ¼ cup of sugar
- ¼ teaspoon red pepper flakes, crushed
- 1-pound haddock steak

Directions:

1. Select "Sauté/Sear" mode of Ninja Foodi and place all ingredients except haddock steak.
2. Press "Start/Stop" to begin and cook for about 3-4 minutes, stirring continuously.
3. In a suitable bowl, reserve half of the marinade.
4. In a resealable bag, add the remaining marinade and haddock steak.
5. Seal the haddock's ziplock bag and shake it well to coat.
6. Refrigerate for about 30 minutes.
7. Arrange the greased Air Fryer Basket into the Ninja Foodi's pot of Ninja Foodi.
8. Close the Ninja Foodi with a crisping lid and select "Air Crisp" mode.
9. Set the temperature to 390 degrees F temperature for almost 5 minutes.
10. Press "Start/Stop" to begin preheating.
11. After preheating, open the lid.
12. Place the haddock steak into the Air Fryer Basket.
13. Close the Ninja Foodi with a crisping lid and select "Air Crisp" mode.
14. Set the temperature to 390 degrees F temperature for almost 11 minutes.
15. Hit the "Start/Stop" button to initiate cooking.
16. Open the lid and transfer the haddock steak onto a serving platter.
17. Immediately coat the haddock steaks with the remaining glaze.
18. Serve immediately.

Nutrition Values Per Serving:

Calories: 192, Total fat: 1.2g, Fiber: 1g, Carbohydrates: 15.1g, Protein: 3.2g

Basil Shrimp Scampi

Prep Time: 15 minutes

Cooking Time: 7 minutes

Servings: 3

Ingredients:

- 4 tablespoons salted butter
- 1 tablespoon fresh lemon juice
- 1 tablespoon garlic, minced
- 2 teaspoons red pepper flakes, crushed
- 1-pound shrimp, peeled and deveined
- 2 tablespoons fresh basil, chopped
- 1 tablespoon fresh chives, chopped

- 2 tablespoons chicken broth

Directions:

1. Toss shrimp with the scampi ingredients in the Ninja Foodi's insert.
2. Close the Ninja Foodi with a crisping lid and select "Air Crisp" mode.
3. Set the temperature to 325 degrees F temperature for almost 7 minutes.
4. Hit the "Start/Stop" button to initiate cooking.
5. Once done, open the lid and serve warm.

Nutrition Values Per Serving:

Calories: 245, Total fat: 16g, Fiber: 0.3g, Carbohydrates: 9g, Protein: 26g

Tuna Bake

Prep Time: 3 minutes

Cooking Time: 10 minutes

Servings: 2

Ingredients:

- 1 can cream-of-mushroom soup
- 1 ½ cups water
- 1 ¼ cups macaroni pasta
- 1 can tuna
- ½ cup frozen peas
- ½ teaspoons salt
- 1 teaspoon pepper
- ½ cup shredded cheddar cheese

Directions:

1. Mix soup and water in Ninja Foodi.
2. Add remaining ingredients except for cheese. Stir.
3. Close Ninja Foodi, press the pressure button, at high, and set the time to 4 minutes.
4. Once done cooking, do a quick release.
5. Remove the pressure lid.
6. Stir in cheese and roast for 5 minutes.
7. Serve and enjoy.

Nutrition Values Per Serving:

Calories: 378, Carbohydrates: 34.0g, Protein: 28.0g, Total fats 14.1g

Butter Dipped Crab Legs

Prep Time: 15 minutes

Cooking Time: 4 minutes

Servings: 2

Ingredients:

- 1½ pounds frozen crab legs
- Salt, as required
- 2 tablespoons butter, melted

Directions:

1. Into the Ninja Foodi's pot of Ninja Foodi, place 1 cup of water and 1 teaspoon of salt.

2. Arrange the "Reversible Rack" into the Ninja Foodi's pot of Ninja Foodi.

3. Place the crab legs over the "Reversible Rack "and sprinkle with salt.

4. Close the Ninja Foodi's pressure lid.

5. Select "Pressure" and set it to "High" for 4 minutes.

6. Hit the "Start/Stop" button to initiate cooking.

7. Once done, quick release the cooker's pressure.

8. Open the lid and transfer crab legs onto a serving platter.

9. Drizzle with butter and serve.

Nutrition Values Per Serving:

Calories: 445, Total fat: 17g, Fiber: 0g, Carbohydrates: 0g, Protein: 65g

Salmon Bake

Prep Time: 5 minutes

Cooking Time: 20 minutes

Servings: 2

Ingredients:

- 1 cup chicken broth
- 1 cup milk
- 1 salmon filet
- 2 tablespoons olive oil
- Ground pepper to taste
- 1 teaspoon minced garlic
- 1 cup of frozen vegetables
- ½ can of cream of celery soup
- ¼ teaspoons dill
- ¼ teaspoons cilantro
- 1 teaspoon Italian spice
- 1 teaspoon poultry seasoning
- 1 tablespoon ground parmesan

Directions:

1. Press the sauté button on Ninja Foodi and add oil to heat.

2. Place the salmon in the heated oil and cook for 2 minutes per side.

3. Stir in garlic, cook for 30 seconds then add broth and cook for 3 minutes.

4. Add the spices, milk, vegetables, noodles and stir.

5. Add the cream of celery soup on top and stir well.

6. Cover the pressure lid. Press the pressure cook button, select high settings and cook for 8 minutes.

7. Once done cooking, do a quick release.

8. Serve and enjoy with a sprinkle of parmesan.

Nutrition Values Per Serving:

Calories: 616, Carbohydrates: 28.7g, Protein: 51.8g, Total fats 32.6g

New Orleans Seafood Gumbo

Prep Time: 5 minutes

Cooking Time: 20 minutes

Servings: 2

Ingredients:

- 1 sea bass filet patted dry and cut into 2" chunks
- 1 tablespoon ghee or avocado oil
- 1 tablespoon Cajun seasoning
- 1 small yellow onion diced
- 1 small bell pepper diced
- 1 celery rib diced
- 2 Roma tomatoes diced
- 1 tablespoon tomato paste
- 1 bay leaf
- ½ cup bone broth
- ¾-pound medium to large raw shrimp deveined
- Sea salt
- Black pepper

Directions:

1. Press the sauté button and heat the oil.
2. Season fish chunks with pepper, salt, and half of Cajun seasoning.
3. When the oil is hot, sear fish chunks for 3 minutes per side and transfer to a plate.
4. Stir in remaining Cajun seasoning, celery, and onions. Sauté for 2 minutes.
5. Stir in bone broth, bay leaves, tomato paste, and diced tomatoes. Mix well. Add back fish.
6. Close Ninja Foodi, press the pressure cook button, select high settings, and set the time to 5 minutes.
7. Once done cooking, do a quick release.
8. Stir in shrimps, cover and cook 5 minutes in the residual heat.
9. Serve and enjoy.

Nutrition Values Per Serving:

Calories: 357, Carbohydrates: 14.8g, Protein: 45.9g, Total fats 12.6g

Tomato Dipped Tilapia

Prep Time: 2 minutes

Cooking Time: 4 minutes

Servings: 2

Ingredients:

- 2 tilapia fillets
- Salt and black pepper
- 2 Roma tomatoes, diced

- 2 minced garlic cloves
- ¼ cup chopped basil, fresh
- 1 tablespoon olive oil
- ¼ teaspoons salt
- 1/8 teaspoons pepper
- 1 tablespoon Balsamic vinegar

Directions:

1. Add a cup of water to Ninja Foodi, place steamer basket, and add tilapia in the basket. Season with pepper and salt.

2. Close Ninja Foodi, press the steam button and set the time to 2 minutes.

3. Mix black pepper, olive oil, salt, basil, garlic, and tomatoes, then mix well.

4. Once done cooking, do a quick release.

5. Serve and enjoy with the basil-tomato dressing.

Nutrition Values Per Serving:

Calories: 196, Carbohydrates: 2.0g, Protein: 20.0g, Total fats 12.0g

Tangy Catfish

Prep Time: 10 minutes

Cooking Time: 13 minutes

Servings: 2

Ingredients:

- 2 tablespoons flour
- 1 teaspoon red chili powder
- ½ teaspoon paprika
- ½ teaspoon garlic powder
- Salt, as required
- 2 (6-ounces) catfish fillets
- 1 tablespoon olive oil

Directions:

1. Arrange the greased Air Fryer Basket into the Ninja Foodi's pot of Ninja Foodi.

2. Close the Ninja Foodi with a crisping lid and select "Air Crisp" mode.

3. Set the temperature to 400 degrees F temperature for almost 5 minutes.

4. Press "Start/Stop" to begin preheating.

5. In a suitable bowl, mix the flour, paprika, garlic powder and salt.

6. Add the catfish fillets and coat with the mixture evenly.

7. Now, coat each fillet with oil.

8. After preheating, open the lid.

9. Place the catfish fillets into the Air Fryer Basket.

10. Close the Ninja Foodi with a crisping lid and select "Air Crisp" mode.

11. Set the temperature to 400 degrees F for almost 13 minutes.

12. Hit the "Start/Stop" button to initiate cooking.

13. Flip the fish fillets once cooked halfway through.

14. Open the lid and serve hot.

Nutrition Values Per Serving:

Calories: 458, Total fat: 34.2g, Fiber: 3.7g, Carbohydrates: 7.5, Protein: 32g

Parmesan Crusted Tilapia

Prep Time: 10 minutes

Cooking Time: 4 hours

Servings: 4

Ingredients:

- ½ cup Parmesan cheese, grated
- ¼ cup mayonnaise
- ¼ cup fresh lemon juice
- Salt and black pepper, as required
- 4 (4-ounce) tilapia fillets
- 2 tablespoons fresh cilantro, chopped

Directions:

1. In a suitable bowl, mix all ingredients except tilapia fillets and cilantro.

2. Coat the fillets with a mayonnaise mixture evenly.

3. Place the filets over a large piece of foil.

4. Wrap the foil around fillets to seal them.

5. Arrange the foil packet at the bottom of Ninja Foodi.

6. Close the Ninja Foodi with a crisping lid and select "Slow Cook".

7. Set on "Low" and cook for 3-4 hours.

8. Hit the "Start/Stop" button to initiate cooking.

9. Remove the lid and transfer the foil parcel onto a platter.

10. Open the parcel and serve hot with the garnishing of cilantro.

Nutrition Values Per Serving:

Calories: 190, Total fat: 8.5g, Fiber: 2g, Carbohydrates: 3.9g, Protein: 25g

Sea Bass Curry

Prep Time: 2 minutes

Cooking Time: 3 minutes

Servings: 2

Ingredients:

- 1 can coconut milk
- Juice, 1 lime
- 1 tablespoon red curry paste
- 1 teaspoon fish sauce
- 1 teaspoon coconut aminos
- 1 teaspoon honey

- 2 teaspoons sriracha
- 2 cloves garlic, minced
- 1 teaspoon ground turmeric
- 1 teaspoon ground ginger
- ½ teaspoon of sea salt
- ½ teaspoon white pepper
- 1-pound sea bass, cut into 1" cubes
- ¼ cup chopped fresh cilantro
- 2 lime wedges

Directions:

1. Mix black pepper, ginger, salt, garlic, sriracha, turmeric, honey, red curry paste, coconut aminos, fish sauce, lime juice, and coconut milk in a suitable bowl.

2. Place fish in the pot and pour coconut milk mixture over it.

3. Close the Ninja Foodi, press the pressure button, at high, and cook for 3 minutes.

4. Once done cooking, do a quick release.

5. Serve and enjoy with equal amounts of lime wedge and cilantro.

Nutrition Values Per Serving:

Calories: 749, Carbohydrates: 16.6g, Protein: 58.0g, Total fats 50.0g

Fish Coconut Curry

Prep Time: 5 minutes

Cooking Time: 15 minutes

Servings: 2

Ingredients:

- 1-lb fish steaks or fillets, rinsed and cut into bite-size pieces
- 1 tomato, chopped
- 1 green chile, julienned
- 1 small onion, julienned
- 2 garlic cloves, squeezed
- ½ tablespoons grated ginger
- 2 bay laurel leaves
- 1 teaspoon ground coriander
- 1 teaspoon ground cumin
- ½ teaspoons ground turmeric
- ½ teaspoons Chilli powder
- ½ teaspoons ground fenugreek
- 1 cup unsweetened coconut milk
- Salt to taste

Directions:

1. Press the sauté button and heat the oil.

2. Add garlic, sauté for a minute. Stir in ginger and onions.

3. Sauté for 5 minutes. Stir in bay leaves, fenugreek, Chilli powder, turmeric, cumin, and coriander.

4. Sauté for 1 minute, then pour in coconut milk to deglaze the pot.

5. Stir in tomatoes and green chilies. Mix well.

6. Add fish and mix well.

7. Cover the pressure lid. Press the pressure cook button, select low settings and cook for 5 minutes.

8. Once done cooking, do a quick release.

9. Serve and enjoy.

Nutrition Values Per Serving:

Calories: 434, Carbohydrates: 11.7g, Protein: 29.7g, Total fats 29.8g

Mixed Seafood Stew

Prep Time: 5 minutes

Cooking Time: 35 minutes

Servings: 2

Ingredients:

- 1 tablespoon vegetable oil
- ½ 14.5-oz can fire-roasted tomatoes
- ½ cup diced onion
- ½ cup chopped carrots
- ½ cup of water
- ½ cup white wine or broth
- 1 bay leaf
- ½ tablespoon tomato paste
- 1 tablespoon minced garlic
- 1 teaspoon fennel seeds toasted and ground
- ½ teaspoon dried oregano
- 1 teaspoon salt
- 1 teaspoon red pepper flakes
- 2 cups mixed seafood
- 1 tablespoon fresh lemon juice

Directions:

1. Press sauté button on Ninja Foodi and heat oil.

2. Once hot, stir in onion and garlic. Sauté for 5 minutes.

3. Stir in tomatoes, bay leaves, tomato paste, oregano, salt, and pepper flakes. Cook for 5 minutes.

4. Stir in bell pepper, water, wine, and fennel seeds. Mix well.

5. Close Ninja Foodi, press the pressure button, select high settings, and set the time to 15 minutes.

6. Once done cooking, do a quick release.

7. Stir in defrosted mixed seafood.

8. Cover and let it cook for 10 minutes in the residual heat.

9. Serve and enjoy with a dash of lemon juice.

Nutrition Values Per Serving:

Calories: 202, Carbohydrates: 10.0g, Protein: 18.0g, Total fats 10.0g

Salmon with Orange Sauce

Prep Time: 3 minutes

Cooking Time: 15 minutes

Servings: 2

Ingredients:

- 1-pound salmon
- 1 tablespoon dark soy sauce
- 2 teaspoons minced ginger
- 1 teaspoon minced garlic
- 1 teaspoon salt
- 1 ½ teaspoons ground pepper
- 2 tablespoons low sugar marmalade

Directions:

1. In a heatproof pan that fits inside your Ninja Foodi, add salmon.

2. Mix all the sauce ingredients and pour over the salmon. Allow marinating for 15-30 minutes. Cover pan with foil securely.

3. Put 2 cups of water in Ninja Foodi and add the trivet.

4. Place the pan of salmon on the trivet.

5. Cover the pressure lid. Press the pressure cook button, select Low settings, and cook for 5 minutes.

6. Once done cooking, do a quick release.

7. Serve and enjoy.

Nutrition Values Per Serving:

Calories: 177, Carbohydrates: 8.8g, Protein: 24.0g, Total fats 5.0g

Herbed Cod Parcel

Prep Time: 15 minutes

Cooking Time: 8 minutes

Servings: 2

Ingredients:

- 2 (4-ounce) cod fillets
- ½ teaspoon garlic powder
- Salt and black pepper, as required
- 2 fresh dill sprigs
- 4 lemon slices
- 2 tablespoons butter

Directions:

1. Place 1 fillet in the center of one parchment square.
2. Drizzle garlic powder, salt and black pepper over each fillet.
3. Top each of these fillets with 2 lemon slices, 1 dill sprig, and 1 tablespoon butter.
4. Fold each parchment paper around the fillets to seal.
5. Into the Ninja Foodi's pot of Ninja Foodi, place 1 cup of water.
6. Arrange the "Reversible Rack" into the Ninja Foodi's pot of Ninja Foodi.
7. Place the fish parcels over the "Reversible Rack".
8. Close the Ninja Foodi pressure lid and place the pressure valve to the "Seal" position.
9. Select "Pressure" and set it to "High for 8 minutes.
10. Hit the "Start/Stop" button to initiate cooking.
11. Once done, release the pressure naturally then remove the lid.
12. Open the lid and transfer the fish parcels onto serving plates.
13. Carefully unwrap the parcels and serve.

Nutrition Values Per Serving:

Calories: 227, Total fat: 12.9g, Fiber: 3g, Carbohydrates: 10.3g, Protein: 22g

Salmon with Dill Sauce

Prep Time: 10 minutes

Cooking Time: 2 hours

Servings: 6

Ingredients:

- 2 cups water
- 1 cup chicken broth
- 2 tablespoons fresh lemon juice
- ¼ cup fresh dill, chopped
- ½ teaspoon lemon zest, grated
- 6 (4-ounce) salmon fillets
- Salt and black pepper, as required

Directions:

1. Into the Ninja Foodi's pot of Ninja Foodi, mix the water, broth, lemon juice, lemon juice, dill and lemon zest.

2. Arrange the prepared salmon fillets on top, skin side down and sprinkle with salt and black pepper.

3. Close the Ninja Foodi with a crisping lid and select "Slow Cook" mode. Set on "Low" for 1-2 hours.

4. Hit the "Start/Stop" button to initiate cooking.

5. Open the lid and serve hot.

Nutrition Values Per Serving:

Calories: 164, Total fat: 7.7g, Fiber: 1g, Carbohydrates: 1.6g, Protein: 23g

Spinach Scallops

Prep Time: 15 minutes

Cooking Time: 15 minutes

Servings: 3

Ingredients:

- 1 (10-ounce) package spinach, drained
- 12 sea scallops
- Olive oil cooking spray
- Salt and black pepper, as required
- ¾ cup heavy whipping cream
- 1 tablespoon tomato paste
- 1 teaspoon garlic, minced
- 1 tablespoon fresh basil, chopped

Directions:

1. Arrange the greased Air Fryer Basket into the Ninja Foodi's pot of Ninja Foodi.
2. Close the Ninja Foodi with a crisping lid and select "Air Crisp" mode.
3. Set the temperature to 350 degrees F temperature for almost 5 minutes.
4. In the bottom of a 7-inch heatproof pan, place the spinach.
5. Spray each scallop with cooking spray and then sprinkle with a little salt and black pepper.
6. Arrange scallops on top of the spinach in a single layer.
7. In a suitable bowl, add the cream, tomato paste, garlic, basil, salt and black pepper and mix well.
8. Place the cream mixture over the spinach and scallops evenly.
9. After preheating, open the lid.
10. Place the pan into Air Fryer Basket.
11. Close the Ninja Foodi with a crisping lid and select "Air Crisp" mode.
12. Set the temperature to 350 degrees F temperature for almost 10 minutes.
13. Hit the "Start/Stop" button to initiate cooking.
14. Open the lid and serve hot.

Nutrition Values Per Serving:

Calories: 234, Total fat: 12.4g, Fiber: 2.3g, Carbohydrates: 8.4g, Protein: 23g

Sweet Mahi-Mahi

Prep Time: 4 minutes

Cooking Time: 10 minutes

Servings: 2

Ingredients:

- 2 6-oz mahi-mahi fillets
- Salt
- Black pepper, to taste
- 1-2 cloves garlic, minced or crushed
- 1" piece ginger, finely grated
- ½ lime, juiced
- 2 tablespoons honey
- 1 tablespoon nana mi togarashi
- 2 tablespoons sriracha
- 1 tablespoon orange juice

Directions:

1. In a heatproof dish that fits inside the Ninja Foodi, mix well orange juice, sriracha, Nanami togarashi, honey-lime juice, ginger, and garlic.

2. Season mahi-mahi with pepper and salt.

3. Place in a bowl of sauce and cover well in the sauce. Seal dish securely with foil.

4. Add a cup of water in Ninja Foodi, place trivet, and add a dish of mahi-mahi on a trivet.

5. Close Ninja Foodi, press the steam button and set the time to 10 minutes.

6. Once done cooking, do a quick release.

7. Serve and enjoy.

Nutrition Values Per Serving:

Calories: 200, Carbohydrates: 20.1g, Protein: 28.1g, Total fats 0.8g

Salmon Pasta

Prep Time: 5 minutes

Cooking Time: 10 minutes

Servings: 2

Ingredients:

- 4 ounces dry pasta
- 1 cup of water
- 3-ounces smoked salmon, broken in bite-sized pieces
- ¼ lemon
- Salt and black pepper
- ½ teaspoon grated lemon zest
- ½ teaspoon lemon juice
- 2 tablespoons heavy cream

- 1 tablespoon walnuts
- 1 clove garlic
- 1 cup packed baby spinach
- 1 ½ tablespoons olive oil
- ¼ cup grated parmesan + more for serving/garnish
- Kosher Salt and black pepper, to taste
- 1 teaspoon grated lemon zest
- ¼ cup heavy cream

Directions:

1. Make the sauce in a blender by pulsing garlic and walnuts until chopped.

2. Add ¼ teaspoons pepper, ¼ teaspoons salt, ½ cup parmesan, oil, and 2/3 of spinach. Puree until smooth.

3. Add butter, water, and pasta in Ninja Foodi.

4. Cover and seal the pressure lid.

5. Close Ninja Foodi, press the pressure button, select high settings, and set the time to 4 minutes.

6. Once done cooking, do a quick release.

7. Press stop and then press sauté.

8. Stir in remaining parmesan, remaining spinach, sauce, lemon juice, lemon zest, heavy cream, and smoked salmon. Mix well and sauté for 5 minutes.

9. Serve and enjoy.

Nutrition Values Per Serving:

Calories: 465, Carbohydrates: 31.0g, Protein: 20.1g, Total fats 29.0g

Buttered Green Peas

Prep Time: 10 minutes

Cooking time: 17 minutes

Servings: 5

Ingredients:

- 2 cups green peas
- ½ cup fresh mint
- 1 tablespoon dried mint
- 1 cup of water
- 1 teaspoon salt
- 1 tablespoon butter
- ½ teaspoon peppercorn
- 1 teaspoon olive oil

Directions:

1. Wash the mint and chop it. Transfer the chopped mint to the Ninja Foodi.
2. Add water and close the Ninja Foodi's lid.
3. Cook the mixture on the "Pressure" mode for 7 minutes.
4. Strain the mint leaves from the water and discard them.
5. Add green peas, dried mint, salt, peppercorn to the liquid into the Ninja Foodi's pot, and Close the Ninja's lid.
6. Cook the dish in the "Pressure" mode for 10 minutes.
7. Rinse the cooked green peas in a colander.
8. Put the peas in the serving bowl and add butter and olive oil.
9. Stir the cooked dish gently until the butter is dissolved.

Nutrition Values Per Serving:

Calories: 97, Total fat: 4.6g, Fiber: 4g, Carbohydrates: 11.48g, Protein: 3g

Turmeric Turnip Fries

Prep Time: 15 minutes

Cooking time: 14 minutes

Servings: 5

Ingredients:

- 1-pound turnips, peeled
- 1 tablespoon avocado oil
- 1 teaspoon dried oregano
- 1 teaspoon onion powder
- ½ teaspoon salt
- 1 teaspoon turmeric

Directions:

1. Cut the turnips into the fries and sprinkle them with the dried oregano, avocado oil, onion powder, and turmeric.

2. Mix the turnip and let it soak the spices for 5-10 minutes.

3. After this, place them in the Ninja basket and Close the Ninja's lid.

4. Set "Air Crisp" cooking mode at 390F and cook the fries for 14 minutes.

5. Stir the turnips fries twice during the cooking.

6. When the meal gets a light brown color, it is cooked.

7. Transfer it to the serving plates and sprinkle it with salt.

Nutrition Values Per Serving:

Calories: 34, Total fat: 0.4g, Fiber: 1.9g, Carbohydrates: 7g, Protein: 0.9g

Sweet Tomato Salsa

Prep Time: 10 minutes

Cooking time: 8 minutes

Servings: 6

Ingredients:

- 2 cups tomatoes, chopped
- 1 teaspoon sugar
- ⅓ cup fresh cilantro
- 2 white onions, chopped
- 1 teaspoon black pepper
- 1 teaspoon cayenne pepper
- ½ jalapeno pepper, chopped
- 1 teaspoon olive oil
- 1 tablespoon minced garlic
- ⅓ cup of green olives
- 1 teaspoon paprika
- ⅓ cup basil
- 1 tablespoon Sugar

Directions:

1. Transfer the vegetables to the Ninja Foodi and sprinkle them with olive oil.

2. Close the Ninja's lid and cook the ingredients on the" Steam" mode for 8 minutes.

3. Meanwhile, wash the tomatoes and chop them.

4. Place the chopped tomatoes in the bowl. Chop the cilantro.

5. Add the chopped cilantro, black pepper, Chilli pepper, and minced garlic in the chopped tomatoes.

6. Add green olives, chop them or leave them whole as desired.

7. Chop the basil and add it to the salsa mixture. Add paprika and olive oil.

8. Once cooked, transfer the veggies from the Ninja Foodi to a plate.

9. Chop the vegetables and add them to the salsa mixture. Sprinkle the dish with Sugar.

10. Mix well and serve.

Nutrition Values Per Serving:

Calories: 41, Total fat: 1.1g, Fiber: 1.9g, Carbohydrates: 7.7g, Protein: 1.2g

Cheesy Dumplings

Prep Time: 10 minutes

Cooking time: 15 minutes

Servings: 6

Ingredients:

- 1 cup cottage cheese
- ½ cup flour
- 1 teaspoon baking soda
- 1 teaspoon salt
- 2 tablespoons Sugar
- 4 tablespoons coconut milk
- 1 teaspoon basil
- 3 eggs

Directions:

1. Blend the cottage cheese in a blender, add eggs and continue blending until smooth.
2. Transfer the mixture to the bowl and add baking soda and flour.
3. Top the mixture with salt, sugar, coconut milk, and basil. Knead the dough.
4. Make the small logs from the dough.
5. Set the Ninja Foodi mode to "Steam," transfer the dough logs to the Ninja Foodi, and Close the Ninja's lid.
6. Cook for 15 minutes. Once it is done, remove the dumplings from the Ninja Foodi.
7. Serve immediately.

Nutrition Values Per Serving:

Calories: 102, Total fat: 6.5g, Fiber: 0.5g, Carbohydrates: 2.6g, Protein: 8.7g

Creamy Asparagus Mash

Prep Time: 6 minutes

Cooking time: 6 minutes

Servings: 1

Ingredients:

- ½ cup asparagus
- ½ cup of water
- 1 tablespoon heavy cream
- 1 tablespoon fresh basil, chopped
- ½ teaspoon salt
- ¾ teaspoon lemon juice

Directions:

1. Put asparagus in the Ninja cooker. Add water and salt.
2. Close and seal the lid. Cook the vegetables on "Pressure" cooking mode for 6 minutes.
3. Open the lid and drain half of the liquid. Add fresh basil.
4. Using the hand blender, blend the mixture until smooth.
5. Then add lemon juice and heavy cream. Stir the mash and transfer it into the serving bowls.

Nutrition Values Per Serving:

Calories: 67, Total fat: 5.7g, Fiber: 1.5g, Carbohydrates: 3.2g, Protein: 1.9g

Eggplant Turnip Casserole

Prep Time: 10 minutes

Cooking time: 20 minutes

Servings: 8

Ingredients:

- 3 eggplants, chopped
- 1 white onion, chopped
- 1 bell pepper, chopped
- 1 turnip, chopped
- 1 teaspoon salt
- 1 teaspoon black pepper
- 1 teaspoon cayenne pepper
- ½ teaspoon white pepper
- 1 cup cream
- 5 oz Parmesan, grated

Directions:

1. Mix white onion, bell pepper, and turnip.
2. Add salt, black pepper, cayenne pepper, and white pepper.
3. In the cooker place, eggplants. Then add the layers of onion mixture.
4. Add cheese and cream. Close and seal the lid.
5. Cook the casserole for 10 minutes on" Pressure" cooking mode.
6. Then make quick pressure release, then serve warm.

Nutrition Values Per Serving:

Calories: 144, Total fat: 6g, Fiber: 8.1g, Carbohydrates: 17.3g, Protein: 8.5g

Turmeric Cauliflower Rice

Prep Time: 10 minutes

Cooking time: 5 minutes

Servings: 2

Ingredients:

- 1 cup cauliflower
- 1 tablespoon turmeric
- ½ teaspoon onion powder

- ½ teaspoon garlic powder
- 1 teaspoon dried dill
- ½ teaspoon salt
- 1 teaspoon butter
- 2 pecans, chopped
- ½ cup of water

Directions:

1. Chop the cauliflower roughly and place it in the food processor.
2. Pulse it 3-4 time or until you get cauliflower rice.
3. After this, transfer the vegetables to the cooker.
4. Add onion powder, garlic powder, dried dill, and salt.
5. Then add chopped pecans and water.
6. Stir the mixture gently with the help of the spoon and Close the Ninja's lid.
7. Cook it on" Pressure" cooking mode for 5 minutes.
8. Then use quick pressure release and open the lid.
9. Drain the water using the colander.
10. Transfer the cauliflower rice to the big bowl, add turmeric and butter.
11. Mix the mixture well. Serve it warm.

Nutrition Values Per Serving:

Calories: 145, Total fat: 12.3g, Fiber: 3.6g, Carbohydrates: 8.1g, Protein: 3.1g

Spicy Green Beans

Prep Time: 10 minutes

Cooking time: 15 minutes

Servings: 8

Ingredients:

- 12 ounces green beans
- 1 teaspoon garlic powder
- 1 teaspoon onion powder
- 4 garlic cloves
- 2 tablespoons olive oil
- 1 teaspoon cayenne pepper
- 1 jalapeno pepper
- 1 teaspoon butter
- ½ teaspoon salt
- 1 cup of water

Directions:

1. Wash the green beans and cut each into two equal parts.
2. Toss the green beans in a suitable mixing bowl.
3. Sprinkle the vegetables with onion powder, Chilli pepper, and salt and stir.
4. Remove all the seeds from the jalapeno and chop finely.
5. Add the chopped jalapeno1 to the green bean's mixture.
6. Peel the garlic and slice it. Mix the sliced garlic with olive oil.
7. Blend the mixture and transfer it to the Ninja Foodi.
8. Add the water and stir. Put the green beans in the Ninja Foodi and Close the Ninja's lid.
9. Set the Ninja Foodi mode to" Sauté," and cook the vegetables for 15 minutes.

10. Once cooked, you should have firm but not crunchy green beans.

11. Remove the green beans from the Ninja Foodi and discard the liquid before serving.

Nutrition Values Per Serving:

Calories: 49, Total fat: 4.1g, Fiber: 1g, Carbohydrates: 3g, Protein: 1g

Green Pepper Tomato Salsa

Prep Time: 7 minutes

Cooking time: 10 minutes

Servings: 5

Ingredients:

- 1 cup tomatoes
- 1 teaspoon cumin
- 1 teaspoon ground coriander
- 1 tablespoon cilantro
- ½ cup fresh parsley
- 1 lime
- 1 sweet green pepper
- 1 red onion
- 1 teaspoon garlic powder
- 1 teaspoon olive oil
- 5 garlic cloves

Directions:

1. Remove the seeds from the sweet green pepper and cut it in half.

2. Peel the onion and garlic cloves. Place the vegetables in the Ninja Foodi and sprinkle them with ½ teaspoon of olive oil.

3. Close the Ninja's lid, and set the Ninja Foodi to" Sauté" mode for 10 minutes.

4. Meanwhile, chop the tomatoes and parsley.

5. Peel the lime and squeeze the juice from it.

6. Mix the lime juice with the chopped parsley, cilantro, ground coriander, and garlic powder and stir well.

7. Sprinkle the chopped tomatoes with the lime mixture.

8. Remove the vegetables from the Ninja Foodi.

9. Rough chop the bell pepper and onions and add the ingredients to the tomato mixture.

10. Mix well and serve.

Nutrition Values Per Serving:

Calories: 38, Total fat: 1.2g, Fiber: 1g, Carbohydrates: 6.86g, Protein: 1g

Bok Choy with Mustard Sauce

Prep Time: 10 minutes

Cooking time: 12 minutes

Servings: 7

Ingredients:

- 1-pound bok choy
- 1 cup of water
- ⅓ cup of soy sauce
- 1 teaspoon salt
- 1 teaspoon red Chilli flakes
- 5 tablespoon mustard
- ⅓ cup cream
- 1 teaspoon cumin seeds

- 1 teaspoon black pepper
- 1 tablespoon butter
- ¼ cup garlic clove

Directions:

1. Wash the bok choy and chop it into pieces.
2. Mix water, soy sauce, salt, Chilli flakes, cumin seeds, and black pepper together.
3. Blend the mixture. Peel the garlic clove and cut into thin slices.
4. Add the butter in the Ninja Foodi and sliced garlic.
5. Set the Ninja Foodi to" Sauté" mode and sauté for 1 minute.
6. Add the cream, soy sauce mixture, and bok choy. Close the Ninja's lid.
7. Set the pot to "Sauté" mode and cook for 10 minutes.
8. Drain the water from the Ninja Foodi and sprinkle the bok choy with the mustard, stirring well.
9. Cook for 2 minutes on the manual mode, then transfer the dish to the serving plate.
10. Enjoy.

Nutrition Values Per Serving:

Calories: 83, Total fat: 4.8g, Fiber: 2.1g, Carbohydrates: 7.4g, Protein: 4.2g

Parmesan Tomatoes

Prep Time: 7 minutes

Cooking time: 7 minutes

Servings: 5

Ingredients:

- 10 ounces big tomatoes
- 7 ounces Parmesan cheese
- ½ teaspoon paprika
- 3 tablespoons olive oil
- 1 tablespoon basil
- 1 teaspoon cilantro
- 1 teaspoon onion powder

Directions:

1. Wash the tomatoes and slice them into thick slices.
2. Spray the Ninja Foodi with olive oil inside.
3. Transfer the tomato slices to the Ninja Foodi.
4. Mix the paprika, basil, and cilantro and mix well.
5. Grate the Parmesan cheese and sprinkle the tomato slices with the cheese and spice mixture.
6. Close the Ninja Foodi's lid and cook on the" Sauté" mode for 7 minutes.
7. Once it is done, open the Ninja Foodi's lid and let the tomatoes rest briefly.
8. Transfer the dish to the serving plate.

Nutrition Values Per Serving:

Calories: 250, Total fat: 19.3g, Fiber: 1g, Carbohydrates: 7.85g, Protein: 12g

Cheesy Zucchini

Prep Time: 10 minutes

Cooking time: 10 minutes

Servings: 6

Ingredients:

- 1-pound yellow zucchini
- 3 tablespoons minced garlic
- ½ cup coconut flour
- 3 tablespoons olive oil
- 3 eggs
- ¼ cup of coconut milk
- 7 ounces Romano cheese
- 1 teaspoon salt

Directions:

1. Wash the zucchini and slice them. Mix the minced garlic and salt and stir the mixture.
2. Mix the minced garlic mixture and zucchini slices and mix well.
3. Add the eggs to the suitable mixing bowl and whisk the mixture.
4. Add coconut milk and coconut flour. Stir it carefully until combined.
5. Grate the Romano cheese and add it to the egg mixture and mix.
6. Pour the olive oil in the Ninja Foodi and preheat it.
7. Dip the sliced zucchini into the egg mixture.
8. Transfer the dipped zucchini to the Ninja Foodi and cook the dish in the" Sauté" mode for 2 minutes on each side.
9. Once cooked, remove it from the Ninja Foodi, drain any excess fat using a paper towel, and serve.

Nutrition Values Per Serving:

Calories: 301, Total fat: 21.6g, Fiber: 5.1g, Carbohydrates: 12.5g, Protein: 16g

Seasoned Deviled Eggs

Prep Time: 15 minutes

Cooking time: 5 minutes

Servings: 7

Ingredients:

- 1 tablespoon mustard
- ¼ cup cream
- 1 teaspoon salt
- 8 eggs
- 1 teaspoon mayonnaise
- ¼ cup dill
- 1 teaspoon ground white pepper
- 1 teaspoon minced garlic

Directions:

1. Put the eggs in the Ninja Foodi and add water.
2. Cook the eggs at high pressure for 5 minutes.
3. Remove the eggs from the Ninja Foodi and chill.
4. Peel the eggs and cut them in half. Remove the egg yolks and mash them.
5. Add the mustard, cream, salt, mayonnaise, ground white pepper, and minced garlic to the mashed egg yolks.
6. Chop the dill and sprinkle the egg yolk mixture with the dill. Mix well until smooth.
7. Transfer this egg yolk mixture to a pastry bag fill the egg whites with the yolk mixture.
8. Serve immediately.

Nutrition Values Per Serving:

Calories: 170, Total fat: 12.8g, Fiber: 0g, Carbohydrates: 2.42g, Protein: 11g

Vegetable Salad with Cheese

Prep Time: 10 minutes

Cooking time: 15 minutes

Servings: 7

Ingredients:

- 2 medium carrots
- 7 ounces turnips
- 1 tablespoon olive oil
- 1 red onion
- 4 garlic cloves
- 5 ounces feta cheese
- 1 teaspoon butter
- 1 teaspoon onion powder
- 1 tablespoon salt
- 1 teaspoon black pepper
- 1 red sweet bell pepper

Directions:

1. Put all the vegetables in the Ninja Foodi and cook them in the "Steam" mode for 15 minutes.
2. Chop the cooked vegetables into small pieces.
3. Mix them in a suitable mixing bowl. Add butter and stir.
4. Top the mixture with onion powder, salt, black pepper.
5. Add feta cheese and add rest of the components to the salad.
6. Mix well and serve.

Nutrition Values Per Serving:

Calories: 107, Total fat: 6.9g, Fiber: 1.6g, Carbohydrates: 8.2g, Protein: 3.8g

Black Peas Pickled Garlic

Prep Time: 10 minutes

Cooking time: 9 minutes

Servings: 12

Ingredients:

- 2 cups garlic
- 1 tablespoon salt
- 1 tablespoon olive oil
- 1 teaspoon fennel seeds
- ½ teaspoon black peas
- 3 cups of water
- 5 tablespoon apple cider vinegar
- 1 teaspoon lemon juice
- 1 teaspoon lemon zest
- 1 tablespoon stevia
- 1 teaspoon red Chilli flakes

Directions:

1. Place the salt, olive oil. Fennel seeds, black peas, lemon juice, lemon zest, stevia, and Chilli flakes in the Ninja Foodi.

2. Add water and stir it. Preheat the liquid on the" Pressure" mode for 5 minutes.
3. Meanwhile, peel the garlic. Put the garlic into the preheated liquid.
4. Add apple cider vinegar and stir the mixture.
5. Close the Ninja's lid and cook the garlic on the" Pressure" mode for 4 minutes.
6. Open the Ninja Foodi's lid and leave the garlic in the liquid for 7 minutes.
7. Transfer the garlic to the liquid into a glass jar, such as a Mason jar.
8. Seal the jar tightly and keep it in your refrigerator for at least 1 day before serving.

Nutrition Values Per Serving:

Calories: 46, Total fat: 1.3g, Fiber: 0.6g, Carbohydrates: 7.7g, Protein: 1.5g

Herbed Radish

Prep Time: 10 minutes

Cooking time: 8 minutes

Servings: 5

Ingredients:

- 3 cups radish, trimmed
- 1 tablespoon olive oil
- 1 tablespoon butter
- 1 teaspoon salt
- 1 teaspoon dried dill

Directions:

1. Cut the radishes into halves and place them into the mixing bowl.
2. Sprinkle them with olive oil, salt, and dried dill.
3. Give a good shake to the vegetables.
4. After this, transfer them to the Ninja cooker and add butter.
5. Close the Ninja's lid and set "Air Crisp" cooking mode.
6. Cook the radishes for 8 minutes at 375F.
7. Stir the radish once cooked half way through.
8. Transfer the radishes to the serving plates and serve them hot.

Nutrition Values Per Serving:

Calories: 56, Total fat: 5.2g, Fiber: 1.1g, Carbohydrates: 2.5g, Protein: 0.5g

Soft Cloud Bread

Prep Time: 15 minutes

Cooking time: 7 minutes

Servings: 4

Ingredients:

- 1 egg
- ¾ teaspoon cream of tartar
- 1 tablespoon cream cheese
- ¾ teaspoon onion powder

- ¾ teaspoon dried cilantro

Directions:

1. Separate egg white from egg yolk and place them into the separated bowls.
2. Whisk the egg white with the cream of tartar until the strong peaks.
3. After this, whisk the cream cheese with the egg white until fluffy.
4. Add onion powder and dried cilantro. Stir gently.
5. After this, carefully add egg white and stir it.
6. Scoop the mixture into the Ninja cooker to get small "clouds" and lower the crisp lid.
7. Cook the bread for 7 minutes at 360 degrees F or until it is light brown.
8. Allow it to cool then serve.

Nutrition Values Per Serving:

Calories: 27, Total fat: 0.2g, Fiber: 0g, Carbohydrates: 0.9g, Protein: 1.6g

Butternut Squash Fries

Prep Time: 10 minutes

Cooking time: 15 minutes

Servings: 5

Ingredients:

- 1-pound butternut squash
- 1 teaspoon salt
- ¼ cup of water
- 2 tablespoons turmeric
- 3 tablespoons peanut oil

Directions:

1. Wash the butternut squash and peel it. Cut the butternut squash into strips.
2. Sprinkle the cubes with salt, turmeric, and peanut oil.
3. Stir the mixture well. Place the butternut squash strips into the Ninja Foodi and set it to" Sauté" mode.
4. Sauté the vegetables for 10 minutes. Stir the mixture frequently.
5. Add water and close the Ninja Foodi's lid.
6. Cook the dish on" Pressure" mode for 5 minutes.
7. Once it is done, the butternut squash cubes should be tender but not mushy.
8. Transfer the dish to the serving plate and rest briefly before serving.

Nutrition Values Per Serving:

Calories: 124, Total fat: 8.3g, Fiber: 3g, Carbohydrates: 13.13g, Protein: 1g

Zucchini Noodles

Prep Time: 10 minutes

Cooking time: 10 minutes

Servings: 6

Ingredients:

- 2 medium green zucchinis
- 1 tablespoon wine vinegar
- 1 teaspoon white pepper
- ½ teaspoon cilantro
- ¼ teaspoon nutmeg
- 1 cup chicken stock
- 1 garlic clove

Directions:

1. Wash the zucchini and use a spiralizer to make the zucchini noodles.
2. Peel the garlic and chop it.
3. Mix the cilantro, chopped garlic clove, nutmeg, and white pepper in a suitable mixing bowl.
4. Sprinkle the zucchini noodles with the spice mixture.
5. Pour the chicken stock in the Ninja Foodi and sauté the liquid on the manual mode.
6. Add the zucchini noodles and wine vinegar and stir the mixture gently.
7. Cook for 3 minutes on the" Sauté" mode.
8. Remove the zucchini noodles from the Ninja Foodi and serve.

Nutrition Values Per Serving:

Calories: 28, Total fat: 0.7g, Fiber: 1g, Carbohydrates: 3.94g, Protein: 2g

Marinated Olives

Prep Time: 10 minutes

Cooking time: 17 minutes

Servings: 7

Ingredients:

- 3 cups olives
- 1 tablespoon red Chilli flakes
- 1 teaspoon cilantro
- ⅓ cup olive oil
- 4 tablespoons apple cider vinegar
- 3 tablespoons minced garlic
- ⅓ cup of water
- 3 garlic cloves
- 1-ounce bay leaf
- ¼ cup of water
- 1 teaspoon clove
- 4 tablespoons lime juice

Directions:

1. Mix the Chilli flakes, cilantro, apple cider vinegar, minced garlic, bay leaf, water, and lime juice in a suitable mixing bowl.
2. Add the chopped garlic to the Chilli flake mixture and sprinkle it with the garlic.
3. Add water and place the mixture in the Ninja Foodi.

4. Close the Ninja's lid and cook it in the" Pressure" mode for 10 minutes.

5. Once it is done, remove the mixture from the Ninja Foodi and transfer it to a sealed container.

6. Add olive oil and olives then cook on Sauté mode for 7 minutes.

7. Serve.

Nutrition Values Per Serving:

Calories: 186, Total fat: 16.9g, Fiber: 4g, Carbohydrates: 10.57g, Protein: 1g

Parsley Carrot Fries

Prep Time: 10 minutes

Cooking time: 18 minutes

Servings: 2

Ingredients:

*   2 carrots, peeled
*   1 teaspoon salt
*   1 tablespoon olive oil
*   1 teaspoon dried parsley

Directions:

1. Cut the carrots into the fries and sprinkle with the salt and dried parsley.

2. Mix well and transfer them into the ninja cooker.

3. Close the Ninja's lid and cook the fries on the "Air Crisp" mode for 18 minutes at 385 degrees F.

4. Once done, remove the Ninja's lid and toss well.

5. Serve.

Nutrition Values Per Serving:

Calories: 85, Total fat: 7g, Fiber: 1.5g, Carbohydrates: 6g, Protein: 0.5g

Soft Cinnamon Bun

Prep Time: 10 minutes

Cooking time: 15 minutes

Servings: 8

Ingredients:

- 1 cup flour
- ½ teaspoon baking powder
- 3 tablespoon Sugar
- 2 tablespoon ground cinnamon
- ½ teaspoon vanilla extract
- 1 tablespoon butter
- 1 egg, whisked
- ¾ teaspoon salt
- ¼ cup almond milk

Directions:

1. Mix the flour, baking powder, vanilla extract, egg, salt, and almond milk.
2. Knead the soft and non-sticky dough.
3. Roll the prepared dough using a rolling pin on a floured surface.
4. Sprinkle dough with butter, cinnamon, and Sugar.
5. Roll the dough into the log and cut the roll into 7 pieces.
6. Spray Ninja Foodi Air Fryer's insert with the cooking spray.
7. Place the cinnamon buns in the basket and Close the Ninja's lid.
8. Cook on the "Bake/Roast" cooking mode and cook the buns for 15 minutes at 355 degrees F.
9. Allow the buns to cool and serve.

Nutrition Values Per Serving:

Calories: 127, Total fat: 10.5g, Fiber: 3g, Carbohydrates: 22g, Protein: 4g

Pumpkin Cupcakes

Prep Time: 7 minutes

Cooking time: 20 minutes

Servings: 5

Ingredients:

- 1 tablespoon butter, melted
- 1 tablespoon pumpkin puree
- 1 teaspoon ground cinnamon
- ¼ teaspoon ground ginger
- 1 egg, beaten
- 3 tablespoon Sugar

- ½ cup flour
- ½ teaspoon baking powder

Directions:

1. Mix butter, cinnamon and all of the ingredients in a suitable mixing bowl.
2. Transfer the mixture into the silicone muffin molds and place in the Ninja Foodi.
3. Cover the Ninja Foodi's lid and Cook on the "Bake/Roast" cooking mode.
4. Cook the muffins for 20 minutes at 330 degrees F.
5. Serve.

Nutrition Values Per Serving:

Calories: 52, Total fat: 4.6g, Fiber: 0.7g, Carbohydrates: 23g, Protein: 1.8g

Pecan Muffins

Prep Time: 10 minutes

Cooking time: 12 minutes

Servings: 6

Ingredients:

- 4 tablespoon butter, softened
- 4 tablespoon coconut flour
- 1 egg, whisked
- 4 tablespoon heavy cream
- ½ teaspoon vanilla extract
- 1 tablespoon pecans, crushed
- 2 tablespoon sugar

Directions:

1. Mix coconut flour, butter, egg, heavy cream, vanilla extract, and sugar in a suitable mixing bowl.
2. Use the hand mixer to mix the mixture until smooth.
3. Pour the smooth batter into the silicone muffin molds.
4. Top every muffin with the pecans and transfer in Ninja Foodi rack.
5. Cover the Ninja Foodi's lid and Cook on the "Bake/Roast" cooking mode.
6. Cook the pecan muffins for 12 minutes at 350 degrees F.
7. Serve!

Nutrition Values Per Serving:

Calories: 170, Total fat: 15.1g, Fiber: 3.6g, Carbohydrates: 31.1g, Protein: 2.8g

Creamy Pumpkin Pie

Prep Time: 10 minutes

Cooking time: 25 minutes

Servings: 6

Ingredients:

- 1 tablespoon pumpkin puree
- 1 cup coconut flour
- ½ teaspoon baking powder
- 1 teaspoon apple cider vinegar
- 1 teaspoon Pumpkin spices

- 1 tablespoon butter
- ¼ cup heavy cream
- 2 tablespoon liquid stevia
- 1 egg, whisked

Directions:

1. Mix with the apple cider vinegar, melted butter, heavy cream, stevia, egg, and baking powder in a suitable mixing bowl.
2. Add pumpkin puree, coconut flour, pumpkin spices and stir the batter until smooth.
3. Pour the batter in the Ninja Foodi basket and cover the Ninja Foodi's lid.
4. Set the "Bake/Roast" cooking mode at 360 degrees F.
5. Cook the pie for 25 minutes.
6. Let the pie chill till room temperature.
7. Serve it.

Nutrition Values Per Serving:

Calories: 127, Total fat: 6.6g, Fiber: 8.1g, Carbohydrates: 28g, Protein: 3.8g

Zesty Cake

Prep Time: 8 minutes

Cooking time: 62 minutes

Servings: 6

Ingredients:

- 1 teaspoon dried mint
- 1 cup coconut flour
- 1 teaspoon baking powder
- ¼ cup Sugar
- 2 eggs, whisked
- ¼ cup heavy cream
- 1 tablespoon butter
- ½ teaspoon lemon zest, grated

Directions:

1. In a suitable mixing bowl, mix all the ingredients.
2. Use the cooking machine to make the soft batter from the mixture.
3. Pour the batter into the Ninja Foodie basket and flatten it well.
4. Close the Ninja Foodi's lid and set "Pressure" cooking mode. Seal the lid.
5. Cook the cake on Low pressure for 55 minutes.
6. Then cover the Ninja Foodi's lid and set "Air Crisp" cooking mode.
7. Cook the cake for 7 minutes more at 400 degrees F.
8. Chill the cake well and serve!

Nutrition Values Per Serving:

Calories: 136, Total fat: 7.2g, Fiber: 8.1g, Carbohydrates: 22g, Protein: 4.7g

Easy Vanilla Custard

Prep Time: 5 minutes

Cooking time: 15 minutes

Servings: 4

Ingredients:

- 3 egg yolks
- 1 cup almond milk
- 1 teaspoon vanilla extract
- 2 tablespoon sugar

Directions:

1. Whisk egg yolk and Sugar.
2. Add vanilla extract and almond milk.
3. Preheat your Ninja Foodi cooker at Sauté/Sear cooking mode at 365 degrees F temperature for 5 minutes
4. Then pour the almond milk mixture and sauté it for 10 minutes.
5. Stir the liquid all the time.
6. Transfer it into the serving jars and leave it for 1 hour in the fridge.
7. Serve it!

Nutrition Values Per Serving:

Calories: 181, Total fat: 17.7g, Fiber: 1.3g, Carbohydrates: 32g, Protein: 3.4g

Chocolaty Lava Cakes

Prep Time: 6 minutes

Cooking time: 8 minutes

Servings: 2

Ingredients:

- 2 eggs, whisked
- 3 tablespoons flax meal
- 2 teaspoons of cocoa powder
- ½ teaspoon baking powder
- 2 tablespoons heavy cream
- Cooking spray

Directions:

1. Spray the cake cups with the cooking spray inside.
2. Mix all the remaining ingredients and pour the mixture into the prepared cups.
3. Cover the cups with foil and place them in Ninja Foodi.
4. Cook on the "Bake/Roast" cooking mode 355 degrees F.
5. Close the Ninja's lid and cook the dessert for 8 minutes.
6. Serve the cooked lava cups hot!

Nutrition Values Per Serving:

Calories: 165, Total fat: 13.9g, Fiber: 3.6g, Carbohydrates: 5.3g, Protein: 8.4g

Cinnamon Vanilla Bites

Prep Time: 10 minutes

Cooking time: 12 minutes

Servings: 5

Ingredients:

- 1 teaspoon ground cinnamon
- 1 cup flour
- ½ teaspoon baking powder
- 1 teaspoon olive oil
- ¼ cup almond milk
- 1 teaspoon butter
- ½ teaspoon vanilla extract
- 1 cup water for cooking

Directions:

1. Mix all the dry ingredients.
2. Then add butter and almond milk to the dry ingredients.
3. Add vanilla extract and olive oil and knead the smooth and non-sticky dough.
4. Make the medium sized balls from the prepared dough and place them in the silicone molds.
5. Pour water in Ninja Foodi Air Fryer's insert.
6. Place the molds on the rack in Ninja Foodi.
7. Close the Ninja's lid and seal it.
8. Set "Pressure" cooking mode at High.
9. Cook the cinnamon bites for 10 minutes on the set mode.
10. Once done, naturally release the pressure for 10 minutes.
11. Then remove the liquid from the basket and cover the Ninja Foodi's lid.
12. Set Air Crisp and cook the bites for 2 minutes more.
13. Serve!

Nutrition Values Per Serving:

Calories: 180, Total fat: 15.2g, Fiber: 2.9g, Carbohydrates: 19g, Protein: 5.1g

Vanilla Coconut Muffins

Prep Time: 7 minutes

Cooking time: 2 minutes

Servings: 4

Ingredients:

- 4 tablespoon coconut flour
- 1 teaspoon coconut shred
- 1 teaspoon vanilla extract
- 1 egg, beaten
- 1 tablespoon sugar
- ¼ teaspoon baking powder
- 1 cup water for cooking

Directions:

1. Whisk coconut flour with all the ingredients in a suitable until lump-free.
2. Add water in the Ninja Foodi Air Fryer insert.
3. Place the batter into the muffin molds and transfer them on the Ninja Foodi rack.
4. Cover the Ninja Foodi's lid and set "Pressure" cooking mode at High.

5. Cook the muffins for 2 minutes. Use the quick pressure release method.

6. Let the muffins cool and serve!

Nutrition Values Per Serving:

Calories: 61, Total fat: 2.9g, Fiber: 3.3g, Carbohydrates: 27g, Protein: 2.5g

Chocolate Brownies

Prep Time: 10 minutes

Cooking time: 5 minutes

Servings: 5

Ingredients:

- 1/3 cup flour
- 1 tablespoon sugar
- ¼ cup heavy cream
- ½ teaspoon vanilla extract
- 3 tablespoons cocoa powder
- 3 tablespoons butter
- 1 oz dark chocolate

Directions:

1. Place the flour in the springform pan and flatten to make the layer.

2. Then place the springform pan into the Ninja Foodi's pot and cover the Ninja Foodi's lid.

3. Cook the flour for 3 minutes at 400 degrees F or until the flour gets a golden color.

4. Meanwhile, mix cocoa powder and heavy cream.

5. Add vanilla extract and Sugar.

6. Remove the flour from Ninja Foodi and chill well.

7. Toss butter and dark chocolate into the Ninja Foodi's pot and cook for 1 minute on Sauté/Sear cooking mode.

8. Stir in the heavy cream mixture.

9. Then add chocolate and flour, mix until smooth.

10. Serve.

Nutrition Values Per Serving:

Calories: 159, Total fat: 14.9g, Fiber: 2.1g, Carbohydrates: 21g, Protein: 2.5g

Raspberry Cake

Prep Time: 10 minutes

Cooking time: 30 minutes

Servings: 10

Ingredients:

- 1 ½ cup coconut flour
- 1 teaspoon baking powder
- 1 teaspoon lemon juice
- ½ cup raspberries
- ¼ cup sugar
- 1 egg, whisked
- 1/3 cup almond milk
- 1 tablespoon butter, melted
- ½ teaspoon vanilla extract

Directions:

1. Mix all the dry ingredients.

2. Then add egg, almond milk, and butter.

3. Add vanilla extract and lemon juice.

4. Stir the mixture well. You have to get a liquid batter.

5. Place the layer of the raspberries in the silicone mold.

6. Pour batter over the raspberries.

7. Place the mold on the rack and insert it into the Ninja Foodi basket.

8. Close the Ninja Foodi's lid and Cook on the "Bake/Roast" cooking mode.

9. Cook the cake for 30 minutes at 350 degrees F.

10. Turn the cake upside down on a plate and transfer it to the serving plate.

11. Enjoy!

Nutrition Values Per Serving:

Calories: 107, Total fat: 4.5g, Fiber: 8.9g, Carbohydrates: 25.1g, Protein: 4.3g

Savory Donuts

Prep Time: 20 minutes

Cooking time: 10 minutes

Servings: 5

Ingredients:

- 1 ½ cup flour
- ½ teaspoon baking soda
- 1 teaspoon vanilla extract
- 1 egg, whisked
- 2 tablespoons sugar
- ½ cup heavy cream

Directions:

1. Mix the whisked egg, heavy cream, sugar, vanilla extract, and baking soda.

2. When the mixture is homogenous, add flour.

3. Stir well and knead the non-sticky dough.

4. Let the dough rest for 10 minutes.

5. After this, roll the dough with the help of the rolling pin into 1 inch thick.

6. Then make the donuts with the help of the cutter.

7. Select the Ninja Foodi "Bake/Roast" cooking mode and set 360 degrees F.

8. Place the donuts in the basket and cover the Ninja Foodi's lid.

9. Cook the donuts for 5 minutes.

10. Chill the donuts well and serve!

Nutrition Values Per Serving:

Calories: 118, Total fat: 11.5g, Fiber: 1g, Carbohydrates: 24g, Protein: 2.7g

Mini Chocolate Cakes

Prep Time: 10 minutes

Cooking time: 22 minutes

Servings: 3

Ingredients:

- 1 tablespoon cocoa powder
- 4 tablespoons flour

- ½ teaspoon vanilla extract
- 1 tablespoon sugar
- 1/3 cup heavy cream
- ¼ teaspoon baking powder
- Cooking spray

Directions:

1. Mix the flour, cocoa powder, heavy cream, sugar, vanilla extract, and baking powder.
2. Use the mixer to make the smooth batter.
3. Spray the silicone molds with the cooking spray inside.
4. Pour the batter into the silicone molds and transfer then in Ninja Foodi Air Fryer's insert.
5. Close the Ninja Foodi's lid and set Bake-Roast Option.
6. Cook the cakes at 255 degrees F temperature for 22 minutes.
7. Serve the dessert chilled!

Nutrition Values Per Serving:

Calories: 108, Total fat: 9.6g, Fiber: 1.6g, Carbohydrates: 32g, Protein: 2.6g

Vanilla Brownie

Prep Time: 10 minutes

Cooking time: 32 minutes

Servings: 6

Ingredients:

- 3 tablespoons sugar
- 1 oz chocolate chips
- 2 eggs, whisked
- ½ teaspoon vanilla extract
- 3 tablespoon butter, melted
- 1 tablespoon flour

Directions:

1. Whisk the melted butter, flour, vanilla extract, and Sugar.
2. Melt the chocolate chips and add them to the butter mixture.
3. Add eggs and stir until smooth.
4. Pour the batter into Ninja Foodi Air Fryer's insert, select "Bake/Roast" cooking mode and cook at 360 degrees F temperature for 32 minutes.
5. Then check if the brownie cooked and chill well.
6. Cut it into the servings and serve!

Nutrition Values Per Serving:

Calories: 99, Total fat: 8.8g, Fiber: 0.1g, Carbohydrates: 19g, Protein: 2.4g

Gingered Cookies

Prep Time: 10 minutes

Cooking time: 14 minutes

Servings: 7

Ingredients:

- 1 cup flour
- 3 tablespoons butter
- 1 egg
- ½ teaspoon baking powder
- 3 tablespoon sugar
- 1 teaspoon ground ginger

- ½ teaspoon ground cinnamon
- 3 tablespoons heavy cream

Directions:

1. Beat the egg in suitable bowl and whisk it gently.
2. Add baking powder, sugar, ground ginger, ground cinnamon, heavy cream, and flour.
3. Stir gently and add butter, then Knead the non-sticky dough.
4. Roll the prepared dough with the help of the rolling pin and make the cookies with the help of the cutter.
5. Place the cookies in the basket in one layer and Close the Ninja's lid.
6. Cook on the "Bake/Roast" cooking mode and cook the cookies for 14 minutes at 350 degrees F.
7. Serve.

Nutrition Values Per Serving:

Calories: 172, Total fat: 15.6g, Fiber: 1.8g, Carbohydrates: 31g, Protein: 4.4g

Cocoa Avocado Mousse

Prep Time: 10 minutes

Cooking time: 2 minutes

Servings: 7

Ingredients:

- 2 avocados, peeled, cored
- 1 teaspoon of cocoa powder
- 1/3 cup heavy cream
- 1 teaspoon butter
- 3 tablespoons sugar
- 1 teaspoon vanilla extract

Directions:

1. Preheat your Ninja Foodi cooker at "Sauté/Sear" cooking mode for 5 minutes.
2. Meanwhile, mash the avocado until smooth and mix it with sugar.
3. Place the butter into the Ninja Foodi's pot and melt.
4. Add mashed avocado mixture and stir well.
5. Add cocoa powder and stir until homogenous. Sauté the mixture for 3 minutes.
6. Meanwhile, whisk the heavy cream at high speed for 2 minutes.
7. Transfer the cooked avocado mash to the bowl and chill in ice water.
8. Add whisked heavy cream and vanilla extract. Stir gently to get swirls.
9. Transfer the mousse into small cups and chill for 4 hours in the fridge.
10. Serve!

Nutrition Values Per Serving:

Calories: 144, Total fat: 13.9g, Fiber: 3.9g, Carbohydrates: 15g, Protein: 1.3g

Sweet Almond Bites

Prep Time: 10 minutes

Cooking time: 14 minutes

Servings: 5

Ingredients:

- 1 egg, whisked
- 1 cup flour

- ¼ cup almond milk
- 1 tablespoon coconut flakes
- ½ teaspoon vanilla extract
- ½ teaspoon baking powder
- ½ teaspoon apple cider vinegar
- 2 tablespoons butter

Directions:

1. Mix the whisked egg, almond milk, baking powder, apple cider vinegar, vanilla extract, and butter.
2. Stir the mixture and add flour and coconut flakes. Knead the dough.
3. Make the medium balls from the dough and place them on the rack of Ninja Foodi.
4. Press them gently with the hand palm.
5. Cover the Ninja Foodi's lid and cook the dessert for 12 minutes at 360 degrees F.
6. Enjoy!

Nutrition Values Per Serving:

Calories: 118, Total fat: 11.5g, Fiber: 1g, Carbohydrates: 2.4g, Protein: 2.7g

Chocolate Chip Cookies

Prep Time: 10 minutes

Cooking time: 9 minutes

Servings: 8

Ingredients:

- 1 oz chocolate chips
- 3 tablespoon butter
- 1 cup flour
- 1 egg, whisked
- 2 tablespoons sugar

Directions:

1. Mix the flour and whisked the egg.
2. Add butter and sugar, and mix the mixture until homogenous.
3. Add chocolate chips and knead the homogenous dough.
4. Make 8 small balls from the dough and transfer them to the rack of Ninja Foodi.
5. Close the Ninja Foodi's lid and Cook on the "Bake/Roast" cooking mode.
6. Cook the chip cookies for 9 minutes at 360 degrees F.
7. Chill the cookies and serve!

Nutrition Values Per Serving:

Calories: 145, Total fat: 12.3g, Fiber: 1.5g, Carbohydrates: 12g, Protein: 3.9g

Blackberry Vanilla Cake

Prep Time: 8 minutes

Cooking time: 20 minutes

Servings: 4

Ingredients:

- 4 tablespoons butter

- 3 tablespoon sugar
- 2 eggs, whisked
- ½ teaspoon vanilla extract
- 1 oz blackberries
- 1 cup flour
- ½ teaspoon baking powder

Directions:

1. Mix all the liquid cake ingredients.
2. Then add baking powder, flour, and Sugar.
3. Stir the mixture until smooth.
4. Add blackberries and stir the batter gently with the help of the spoon.
5. Take the non-sticky springform pan and transfer the batter inside.
6. Place the springform pan into the Ninja Foodi's pot and cover the Ninja Foodi's lid.
7. Cook the cake for 20 minutes at 365 degrees F.
8. Chill it and serve!

Nutrition Values Per Serving:

Calories: 173, Total fat: 16.7g, Fiber: 1.1g, Carbohydrates: 32g, Protein: 4.2g

Zucchini Crisps

Prep Time: 5 minutes

Cooking time: 10 minutes

Servings: 4

Ingredients:

- 1 zucchini, chopped
- 1 teaspoon Vanilla extract
- 2 tablespoon sugar
- 1 tablespoon coconut flakes
- 2 tablespoon butter
- 1 tablespoon flour

Directions:

1. Preheat your Ninja Foodi cooker at Sauté/Sear cooking mode for 5 minutes at 360 degrees F.
2. Toss the butter in the Ninja Foodi Air Fryer insert.
3. Add chopped zucchini and Sauté the vegetables for 3 minutes.
4. Add vanilla extract, coconut flakes, Sugar, and stir well.
5. Cook the zucchini for 4 minutes more.
6. Then add flour and stir well.
7. Sauté the dessert for 1 minute.
8. Cook on the "Air Crisp" cooking mode for 2 minutes to get a crunchy crust.
9. Serve the cooked dessert immediately!

Nutrition Values Per Serving:

Calories: 84, Total fat: 8.5g, Fiber: 0.5g, Carbohydrates: 26g, Protein: 0.3g

Creamy Coconut Pie

Prep Time: 6 minutes

Cooking time: 10 minutes

Servings: 4

Ingredients:

- 1 tablespoon coconut flour
- 5 oz coconut, shredded
- ½ teaspoon vanilla extract
- 1 tablespoon sugar
- 1 teaspoon butter
- 1 egg, whisked
- ¼ cup heavy cream

Directions:

1. Mix the coconut flour, coconut shred, and butter.
2. Stir the mixture until homogenous.
3. Add the whisked egg, vanilla extract, Sugar, and heavy cream. Stir well.
4. Transfer the pie mixture into the basket and cover the Ninja Foodi's lid.
5. Cook on the "Bake/Roast" cooking mode 355 degrees F.
6. Cook the pie for 10 minutes.
7. Check if the pie is cooked with the help of the toothpick and chill it tills the room temperature.
8. Serve it!

Nutrition Values Per Serving:

Calories: 185, Total fat: 16.9g, Fiber: 3.9g, Carbohydrates: 22g, Protein: 3g

Cashew Butter Cookies

Prep Time: 10 minutes

Cooking time: 11 minutes

Servings: 7

Ingredients:

- 1 tablespoon sugar
- 1 egg, whisked
- 6 oz cashew butter

Directions:

1. Mix all the ingredients and make the small balls.
2. Place the balls in the basket of Ninja Foodi and Close the Ninja's lid.
3. Cook on the "Bake/Roast" cooking mode and cook the cookies at 330 degrees F temperature for 11 minutes.
4. Serve!

Nutrition Values Per Serving:

Calories: 152, Total fat: 12.6g, Fiber: 0.5g, Carbohydrates: 18g, Protein: 5.1g

Mini Vanilla Cheesecakes

Prep Time: 30 minutes

Cooking time: 4 minutes

Servings: 4

Ingredients:

- 8 tablespoons cream cheese
- 4 tablespoon sugar
- 2 tablespoons heavy cream
- ½ teaspoon vanilla extract
- 4 tablespoons flour

Directions:

1. Whisk the cream cheese and heavy cream in a suitable mixing bowl.
2. Add vanilla extract and stir again.
3. Scoop the medium balls from the cream cheese mixture.
4. Mix the flour and all the remaining Sugar.
5. Then coat every cheesecake ball into the flour mixture.
6. Freeze the prepared balls for 20 minutes or until they are solid.
7. Place the cheesecake balls in the Ninja Foodi basket and cover the Ninja Foodi's lid.
8. Cook the dessert at 400 degrees F temperature for 4 minutes.
9. Enjoy.

Nutrition Values Per Serving:

Calories: 139, Total fat: 13.1g, Fiber: 0.8g, Carbohydrates: 23g, Protein: 3.2g

Creme Brulee

Prep Time: 20 minutes

Cooking time: 10 minutes

Servings: 3

Ingredients:

- 1 cup heavy cream
- 4 egg yolks
- 3 tablespoons sugar
- ½ teaspoon vanilla extract

Directions:

1. Beat egg yolks with 2 tablespoons sugar in a suitable bowl.
2. Add heavy cream and stir until homogenous.
3. Place the mixture into the ramekins and cover them with the foil.
4. Make the small holes on the top of the foil with the help of the toothpick.
5. Pour ½ cup of water into Ninja Foodi basket and insert trivet.
6. Place the ramekins on the trivet and close the Ninja Foodi's lid.
7. Cook the dessert on "Pressure" cooking mode at High for 10 minutes.

8. Then make the quick pressure release for 5 minutes.

9. Let the dessert chill for 10 minutes.

10. Remove the foil from the ramekins and sprinkle the creme Brulee with Sugar.

11. Use the hand torch to caramelize the surface.

12. Serve it!

Nutrition Values Per Serving:

Calories: 212, Total fat: 20.8g, Fiber: 0g, Carbohydrates: 37g, Protein: 4.4g

Pumpkin Pudding

Prep Time: 10 minutes

Cooking time: 25 minutes

Servings: 4

Ingredients:

- 3 eggs, whisked
- ½ teaspoon vanilla extract
- 4 tablespoons pumpkin puree
- 1 teaspoon pumpkin pie spices
- 1 cup heavy cream
- 2 tablespoon sugar
- 1 cup water for cooking

Directions:

1. Whisk the eggs, pumpkin puree, vanilla extract, pumpkin pie spices, cream, and Sugar.

2. Pour the liquid into the non-stick cake pan.

3. Pour water into the Ninja Foodi's pot.

4. Place the pudding in a cake pan into the Ninja Foodi's pot on the rack and Close the Ninja's lid.

5. Select Steam mode and cook the dessert for 25 minutes.

6. Let the cooked pudding rest for 10 minutes then open the lid.

7. Place it in the fridge for a minimum of 4 hours.

8. Enjoy!

Nutrition Values Per Serving:

Calories: 159, Total fat: 14.5g, Fiber: 0.5g, Carbohydrates: 27g, Protein: 5g

Conclusion

Say goodbye to uneven cooking or burning of the food. Ninja Food container has this special crisper basket which keeps the food off from the base. You get to steam, sauté, sear, air-fry and even bake the cakes and bread inside a Ninja Foodi. These are many options which are rarely combined into a single appliance. But with Ninja Foodi these are all available right at one place. The device comes in many sizes and varieties, which makes it quite suitable for personal and professional use. It's not just the people living in families who find this device most efficient and effective but it can greatly assist the young students living by themselves or all the kitchen newbies, who are not familiar with all the cooking techniques. Now they can rely on this new appliance with complete ease. Let this Foodi bring innovation to your Kitchen shelves and enjoy the best of the crispy meals right at home. Try all over exclusive Ninja Foodi recipes and enjoy the most of it!